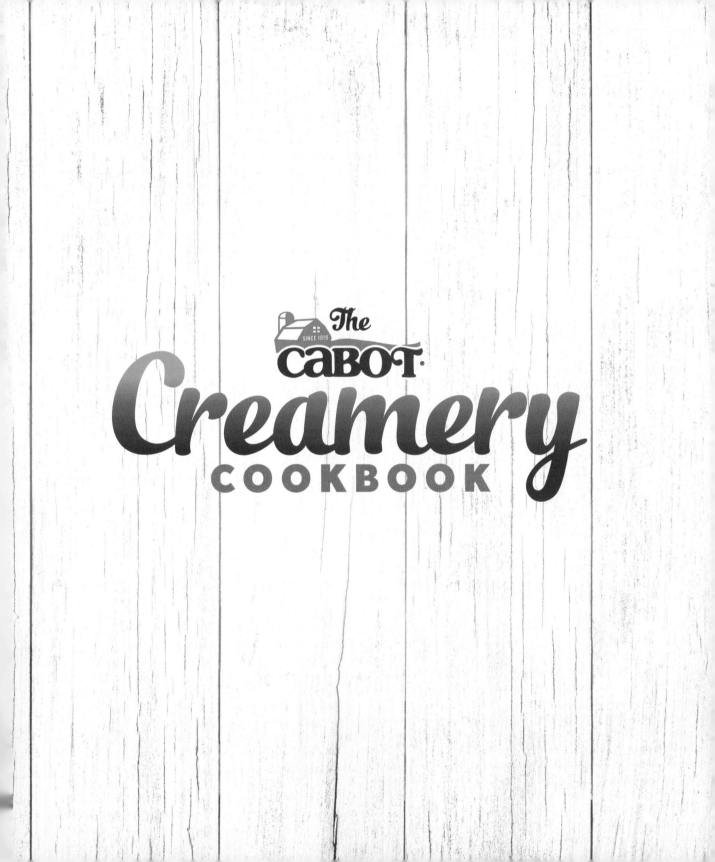

The CABOT® Creamery COOKBOOK

SINCE 1919

The CABOT Creamery COOKBOOK

SIMPLE, WHOLESOME DISHES FROM AMERICA'S BEST DAIRY FARMS

contents

Welcome to Home Cooking!

MY EXPERIENCE AS HOST of "Neighborhood Kitchens" for Boston's WGBH has led me to believe that people have strong memories when it comes to family meals. Whether it's that best-in-the-world lasagna or a well-intentioned, if a tad dry, roast chicken, meals remind us of the people and places we love.

A favorite memory of mine, besides square dancing with my grandfather at the Young-at-Heart Club, was picking fresh raspberries with him in Springfield, Massachusetts. While we worked outside, Grandpa's wife, Gert, would make almost every meal from scratch, using ingredients from the garden and from our catch.

Growing up in New York, I remember Cabot cheese was always in our pantry. I frequently requested "macaroni and cheese with chuletas (pork chops)" for my birthday dinner. My mother would use a mixture of sharp and extra sharp Cabot Cheddar, and top the dish with decorative homegrown tomato slices. Even today, when I visit my parents, our most frequent cocktail-hour appetizer is Cabot's Private Stock Cheddar— it's a delicious and perfect cheese for guests, with its bold, sharp taste and crumbly texture. I now live in New England, and Cabot cheeses are still some of my favorites.

I'm not the only one who grew up with Cabot, as you'll see from the wonderful stories and recipes on the following pages. They reflect the heritage of the 1,200 farm families in the nearly 100-year-old Cabot Cooperative. Many of these wholesome family meals use ingredients available on the farm and in season. For example, Missisquoi Valley Farm's mouthwatering Maple Cheesecake includes dairy from their herd and syrup from their maple sugar operation. Wheeler Farm's Summer Squash and Sausage Casserole makes delicious use of their family garden bounty as well.

As for comfort food recipes, this book abounds with options. I like Laurel Brook Farm's Baked Chicken and Rice with Mushrooms and Cheddar in particular. From the many yummy grilled cheese and macaroni and cheese recipes to the elegant Kalamata-Stuffed Chicken with Creamy Roasted Pepper Sauce, there is something here for everyone. These are family meals at their best—where nothing is complicated, but everything is special. Enjoy!

– Margarita Martinez

Cabot takes the responsibility of caring for the animals and land very seriously.

What We Stand For

Every farm in our cooperative is a family farm.

THE CABOT FARMERS' COOPERATIVE CREAMERY was born soon after the turn of the 20th century, when 94 farmers around the town of Cabot in central Vermont joined together to turn their surplus milk into butter. Each contributed $5 per cow and one cord of wood to fuel the cooperative venture, which purchased the local creamery and started, literally, churning out butter and shipping it down to Boston.

By 1930, the farmer-owners decided to expand to Cheddar and hired a cheesemaker. The group continued growing, reaching 600 farming families by 1960. In 1989, Cabot won the first of many blue ribbons against national and then international competition for its cheeses, butter, and other products. A few years later, in 1992, Cabot merged with Agri-Mark, another dairy co-op in southern New England, whose founding predates Cabot's by just one year. Today Cabot is one of three brands of the Agri-Mark Cooperative, which is 1,200 farms strong across all six New England states and New York, employing 600 with four processing plants in Vermont, Massachusetts, and New York.

The Cabot Cooperative has been owned by dairy farmers since 1919.

WE ARE FAMILY From a Massachusetts farm that has been in the same family since 1752 to a farm in New Hampshire started by two sisters about a decade ago, every farm in our cooperative is a family farm. Herd sizes are very small compared to those in other parts of the country—our average member milks less than 140 cows.

WE ARE A COOPERATIVE For nearly 100 years, Cabot Creamery has been committed to returning 100% of profits to the farm family owners whose stewardship provides employment to hundreds, sustains the land, and safeguards our heritage of family farming.

WE ARE YOUR NEIGHBORS We're part of an ever more rare breed of dairy producers in the Northeast that are locally owned and operated, reliant on our local communities for their support, and supportive of them in return. We are good stewards of the land and our animals, putting into motion sustainable innovations to benefit the land, improve animal care, and enrich communities on behalf of our families and consumers. We are involved in our towns. We'll help you dig your car out of a snowy bank and lend you a cup of milk anytime.

Our dairy experts love nothing more than to come up with new and delicious ways to create wonderful-tasting ingredients.

Contented dairy cows are more productive. For the same reasons, we work hard to treat our land right. We have collaborated with the Manomet Center for Conservation Sciences to create the Vital Capital Index for Dairy Agriculture (VCI), for dairy farmers. Our family farms are involved in programs like Cow Power, offered by Vermont's Green Mountain Power, which extracts clean electricity from cow manure.

WE BELIEVE IN THE NEXT GENERATION OF FARMERS We are involved in hands-on education for the general public and the next generation of farmers. Almost all of us grew up participating in 4-H, the national youth development program, and many of us continue to lead local clubs. Among our member farms is a hands-on high school agricultural program at Alvirne School Farm in Hudson, New Hampshire, and Bristol County Agricultural High School in Dighton, Massachusetts. Other programs are the working farm at the renowned Billings Farm and Museum in Woodstock, Vermont, and student-managed herds at the University of Connecticut in Storrs and University of Vermont in Burlington. Many of our members host an annual Open Farm Sunday in the fall. These are free, neighborly welcome events where you'll meet the family and the animals, and you might even be asked to help with farm chores.

WE MAKE DELICIOUS, WHOLESOME FOOD Our dairy experts love nothing more than to come up with new and delicious ways to create wonderful-tasting ingredients, like cheeses, yogurts, butters, and other dairy delights for you out of the fresh milk produced on our farms. In addition to our "World's Best Cheddar," we have developed award-winning lighter versions of sharp Cheddar and creamy Greek-style yogurts. We have also crafted delectable flavored Cheddars, from addictive Horseradish to summery Tomato Basil and even Smoky Bacon. Finally, there's our spicy number one bestseller, Hot Habanero.

Let's get cooking!

David, Beth, and Bob Kennett of Liberty Hill Farm in Rochester, Vermont

Liberty Hill Farm's
Greek-Style Yogurt
and Fruit Pancakes,
page 42

Daybreak

A FARMER'S BREAKFAST

"There's nothing like the sight of steam rising from the sugarhouse when I carry over a hearty breakfast for the crew that has worked a long night boiling sap. We feed our help well."

—Karen Wheeler, Wheeler Farm, Wilmington, Vermont

APPLE, CRANBERRY, AND CHEDDAR MUFFINS

These muffins are nicely balanced sweet-savory breakfast treats with a lovely tender crumb, thanks to the unusual use of cranberry juice in the batter. Many don't realize that Cheddar doesn't have lactose, so these are also lactose free.

2 cups all-purpose flour

⅓ cup sugar

1 Tbsp. baking powder

½ tsp. table salt

1 cup (4 oz.) shredded sharp Cheddar

¾ cup sweetened cranberry juice

⅓ cup canola or vegetable oil

1 large egg

1 cup peeled and finely diced apple (about 1 large apple)

½ cup dried sweetened cranberries

PREHEAT oven to 400°. Coat a 12-cup muffin pan with cooking spray or line with paper or aluminum foil baking cups.

WHISK together flour, sugar, baking powder, and salt in a large mixing bowl. Stir in shredded Cheddar.

WHISK together cranberry juice, oil, and egg in a small bowl. Add juice mixture to dry ingredients along with apple and cranberries, and stir just until dry ingredients are moistened.

SPOON batter into cups, filling two-thirds full. Bake 15 to 20 minutes or until golden brown on top and a wooden pick inserted in center comes out clean. Cool in pan on a wire rack 5 minutes. Remove from pan to wire rack, and cool completely.

MAKES 12 muffins

WHOLE GRAIN GET-UP-AND-GO BARS

1¼ cups uncooked rolled oats

1 cup chopped dried fruit, such as strawberries, cherries, blueberries, or sweetened cranberries

¾ cup firmly packed brown sugar

½ cup whole wheat flour, preferably pastry flour

½ cup sliced almonds or sunflower seed kernels

¼ cup wheat germ or ground flax seed

2 large egg whites

¾ cup 2% reduced-fat Greek-style yogurt, vanilla or fruit flavored

2 Tbsp. butter, melted

½ tsp. vanilla or almond extract

PREHEAT oven to 350°. Coat an 8- or 9-inch square baking dish with cooking spray.

STIR together oats, dried fruit, brown sugar, whole wheat flour, almonds or sunflower seed kernels, and wheat germ or ground flax seed in a large bowl.

LIGHTLY beat egg whites in a small bowl. Whisk yogurt, melted butter, and vanilla or almond extract into egg whites. Stir wet ingredients into dry ingredients until combined well.

SPREAD mixture evenly in prepared baking dish. Bake 20 to 30 minutes or until center is set and top is lightly browned. Cool in pan on a wire rack. Cut into bars.

MAKES 16 to 25 bars, depending on size

These chewy, dense, energy-rich bars are packed with protein and whole grains. They travel well, too, making them great for hikes, lunchboxes, and breakfasts on the move.

Missisquoi Valley Farm
WESTFIELD, VERMONT

FARM FAMILY:
Pauline and
Jacques Couture

YEARS OWNED:
45 [since 1970]

FARMSTEAD:
More than 385 acres

HERD:
130 Holsteins
with a few Holstein-
Angus crosses

**OTHER FARM
BUSINESS:**
Bed and breakfast,
maple syrup products,
grass-fed beef

AWARDS:
2014 Outstanding
Vermont Sugar Makers
of the Year, Green
Pastures Vermont
Dairy Farm of the Year
2004, Jacques was
inducted into the
International Maple
Hall of Fame in 2014

BARN CATS ARE A DIME A DOZEN on a dairy farm, but at Missisquoi Valley Farm you might spy Shelly, the barn duck. Hatched by Pauline and Jacques Couture's grandsons as a school project, Shelly is at home strolling among the Holsteins. Like "the girls," as the Coutures refer to their cows, Shelly is part of the family.

Pauline and Jacques grew up on neighboring dairy farms in Vermont's Northeast Kingdom region, but Pauline was determined to become a "city girl," and headed off to Burlington. Jacques, on the other hand, always knew farming was for him: "As far back as I can remember, I've loved the woods, the cattle, the fields. I really connect with nature." Eventually, Pauline returned home. After the couple married, they took over the family farm. Pauline smiles at the memory and then points out that she made it clear from the start: "I don't do barn."

She does plenty else to keep the farm thriving, including running the bed and breakfast and working on the farm's online maple products business. The Coutures, who recently celebrated their 45th anniversary, are leaders in the Vermont Maple Sugar Makers Association and were named 2014 outstanding sugar makers of the year. Together they raised six children, sharing their rich French-Canadian heritage by speaking French at home and keeping traditions like the festive New Year's Reveillon celebration.

Fall is a particularly busy and beautiful time at Missisquoi Valley Farm, with leaf-peeping tourists and the cows coming in from summer spent on pasture. Jacques and his crew batten down the hatches on all the feed produced over the growing season. "There's such satisfaction in looking at all we've grown right here for our girls," Jacques says about his milking herd. "The last thing I do before going to bed at night, I come check on them. They're part of the family."

Pauline, meanwhile, is a gracious and warm hostess to guests staying in rooms filled with family antiques and her handmade quilts. She cooks up farm-fresh eggs, pancakes, waffles, and maybe her quick maple-cinnamon rolls, happy to see the kitchen table full again. "It's just fun to have guests from all over the world and put life back into the house," she says. "You don't hug the lady behind the counter at the Hampton Inn."

Jacques Couture
and his barn duck, Shelly

Missisquoi Valley Farm's
QUICK MAPLE-CINNAMON ROLLS

Filling

¾ cup firmly packed light brown sugar

¼ cup butter, softened

2 Tbsp. pure maple syrup

1 tsp. ground cinnamon

⅛ tsp. ground nutmeg

Dough

3 cups all-purpose flour

1 Tbsp. baking powder

1 tsp. table salt

½ cup butter, cut into small pieces

1 cup milk

Glaze

2 Tbsp. cream cheese, softened

2 Tbsp. plain Greek-style yogurt

½ cup powdered sugar

PREHEAT oven to 375°. Prepare filling: Stir together brown sugar, ¼ cup butter, maple syrup, cinnamon, and nutmeg until blended.

PREPARE DOUGH: Butter a 9-inch round cake pan. Line bottom of pan with parchment paper; butter parchment paper. Whisk together flour, baking powder, and salt in a medium bowl. Cut ½ cup butter into flour mixture with a pastry blender or fork until crumbly. Add milk, stirring just until dry ingredients are moistened.

TURN dough out onto a floured surface, and knead lightly 3 or 4 times. Roll dough into a 16- x 12-inch rectangle. Spread filling over dough, leaving a ½-inch border.

ROLL dough up, jelly-roll fashion, starting with long side; cut into 12 slices. Beginning in center, place rolls in prepared pan.

BAKE 30 minutes or until golden brown. Cool in pan on a wire rack 5 minutes.

MEANWHILE, PREPARE GLAZE: Beat cream cheese and yogurt at medium speed with an electric mixer until smooth. Add powdered sugar, and beat at low speed until blended; spread over warm rolls.

MAKES 1 dozen rolls

Farmer Pauline Couture often bakes maple-sweetened breads and muffins or these quick cinnamon rolls filled with crushed maple sugar from the family's extensive sugaring operation. We've used a combination of brown sugar and real maple syrup as a substitute for crushed maple sugar.

SPICED BANANA BREAD

Farmers never waste anything. For example, overripe bananas are always a good excuse to bake up a spice-laden loaf of banana bread.

1½ cups all-purpose flour, plus more for dusting

1½ tsp. baking powder

½ tsp. baking soda

½ tsp. table salt

1 tsp. ground cinnamon

1 tsp. ground ginger

¼ tsp. ground nutmeg

2 large eggs

5 Tbsp. butter, melted

1 cup mashed very ripe bananas (about 3 bananas)

1 cup sugar

½ cup plain Greek-style yogurt

2 tsp. vanilla extract

PREHEAT oven to 350°. Coat an 8½- by 4½-inch loaf pan with cooking spray, and then dust with flour.

WHISK together 1½ cups flour, baking powder, baking soda, salt, cinnamon, ginger, and nutmeg in a medium bowl.

WHISK eggs in a medium bowl, and then beat in butter, bananas, sugar, yogurt, and vanilla until smooth. Beat in dry ingredients just until combined. Scrape batter into prepared pan, smoothing top.

BAKE 55 to 65 minutes or until a long wooden pick inserted in center comes out clean. Cool in pan on a wire rack 10 minutes. Remove from pan to wire rack, and cool completely.

MAKES 1 loaf, about 16 slices

Ocean Breeze Farm

WESTERLY, RHODE ISLAND

From left: Standing in rear: Harrison Chagnon (Frank Panciera's grandson) and Brian Aiello (Sylvia Panciera's fiancé); sitting in front: Sylvia Panciera, Frank Panciera, and Lincoln Chagnon (grandson)

WHEN THEY GET UP AT 4:30 IN THE MORNING to milk, the Pancieras can often hear the ocean waves beyond the salt ponds that border their fields. It is one of the few things that have not changed since 1938 when Frank Panciera's parents bought the small farm a mile from the coast. When Frank was growing up, his family had 18 cows and raised 5,000 meat birds in a long barn, which now houses young animals. "We bottled and peddled milk door to door," Frank says. They also took milk in cans to local dairies for distribution. "There were three dairies in Westerly alone." But the dairy industry changed, development pressure grew, and now Ocean Breeze is the only dairy farm that remains, bordered by picturesque rock walls among vacation homes. "It's kind of sad when you're the only one left," Frank observes matter-of-factly.

Ocean Breeze is also for sale, although the Pancieras have conserved the land so it will stay in agriculture. "I didn't want to see it built into houses. My parents worked it all their lives," says Frank. "I don't picture dairy here in 15 to 20 years, but it needs to stay some type of farm, maybe greenhouse vegetables or grass-fed beef. This is good soil." Now in his mid-60s, he milks about 25 cows and crops 100 acres with the help of his daughter Sylvia, who shares his love of animals. "She was the first kid to have a grand champion cow in Eastern States," Frank says, referring to the prestigious regional agricultural show. Although Sylvia's teenage daughter and Frank's other grandkids spend time on the farm, the next generation does not seem interested in taking over.

Sylvia thinks they could open a homemade ice-cream stand to take advantage of all the summer visitors, but her father is not enthusiastic. He has simple taste in food, he says; milk and rice soup made with butter and salt and pepper is a favorite. From his own childhood, he remembers fresh basket cheese, a tradition of his Italian roots, often used to make egg frittatas. Sylvia is involved with the Connecticut dairy council, and she enjoys cooking and attending fairs, where she hands out cheese samples, maple milkshakes, slices of her rich Raspberry-Cream Cheese Coffee Cake, and crackers topped with hot corn-and-Cheddar dip.

Meanwhile, the summer ocean fog continues to roll in, as the herd of black-and-white Holsteins sprinkled with a few red-and-white Holsteins and Jerseys heads out for exercise "every day unless there's a blizzard," Frank says. Sylvia ribs her dad about the golf clubs that are now gathering dust in the old milk room waiting for him to try them out. "There's always something to do on the farm," Frank says.

FARM FAMILY:
Frank Panciera with daughter Sylvia Panciera

YEARS OWNED:
77 [since 1938]

FARMSTEAD:
About 160 acres, including leased and wooded land

HERD:
60 mixed black-and-white and red-and-white Holsteins and a few Jerseys

OTHER FARM BUSINESS:
Firewood

AWARDS:
Green Pastures Rhode Island Dairy Farm of the Year [repeat winner]

Ocean Breeze Farm's
RASPBERRY-CREAM CHEESE COFFEE CAKE

Farmer Sylvia Panciera of the Ocean Breeze Farm loves to bake, and she especially enjoys making this unusual cream cheese-filled coffee cake with a buttery almond-crumb and raspberry jam topping for special events like fairs and smaller occasions like brunches for baby or wedding showers.

2¼ cups all-purpose flour, plus more for dusting

1 cup sugar, divided

¾ cup cold butter, cut up

1 cup sour cream

1 tsp. almond extract

½ tsp. baking powder

½ tsp. baking soda

¼ tsp. table salt

1 large egg

1 (8-oz.) package cream cheese, softened

1 large egg

½ cup seedless raspberry preserves

½ cup sliced almonds

PREHEAT oven to 350°. Butter and flour a 9-inch springform pan. Whisk together 2¼ cups flour and ¾ cup sugar in a large bowl. Cut butter into flour mixture with a pastry blender or fork until crumbly. Reserve 1 cup crumb mixture for topping.

ADD sour cream, almond extract, baking powder, baking soda, salt, and 1 egg to remaining crumb mixture, stirring until blended and a loose dough forms. Using a rubber spatula or back of a wooden spoon, spread dough over bottom and about 2 inches up sides of prepared pan to form a bowl shape.

BEAT cream cheese, remaining ¼ cup sugar, and remaining 1 egg at medium speed with an electric mixer until smooth; pour into center of dough in pan. Spoon preserves in small dollops over cream cheese mixture. Add almonds to reserved crumb mixture, tossing well. Sprinkle almond mixture over top.

BAKE 1 hour to 1 hour and 10 minutes or until filling is set and cake is deep golden brown. Cool cake in pan on a wire rack 15 minutes. Run a knife around edge of cake to loosen; remove sides of pan. Serve warm or at room temperature. Store leftovers in refrigerator.

MAKES 12 servings

TIP>> To soften an 8-oz. package of cream cheese in the microwave, cut it into 1-inch cubes, place it in a micro-wave-safe bowl, and heat on HIGH for 15 to 20 seconds.

RED PEPPER AND CHEDDAR EGG CUPS

2   large red bell peppers

1   tsp. olive oil

⅓   cup chopped onion

2   small cloves garlic, minced

¾   cup (3 oz.) shredded extra sharp Cheddar or flavored Cheddar such as chipotle, habanero, or tomato-basil, plus more for garnish

2   Tbsp. chopped Italian parsley or cilantro

4   large eggs

PREHEAT oven to 400°. Cut peppers in half lengthwise. Pull out and discard seeds and membranes. Cook peppers in a large pan of boiling water until just tender but not collapsed, about 6 minutes. Drain well. Place peppers, cut sides up, in an 8-inch square or similar baking dish. Cool slightly.

HEAT oil in a small skillet set over medium heat. Add onion to skillet and cook, stirring occasionally, 4 to 5 minutes or until softened. Add garlic and cook, stirring frequently, until fragrant. Scrape onion mixture into a small bowl. Cool several minutes, and then stir in Cheddar and parsley or cilantro.

DIVIDE cheese mixture among peppers, pressing mixture up sides of peppers to create a hollow for egg in center of each. Break 1 egg into each pepper half. Sprinkle with salt and pepper.

BAKE 20 minutes or until eggs are cooked to your liking. Sprinkle with a little more cheese, if using, and serve hot.

MAKES 4 servings

KITCHEN WISDOM To break an egg, hold it between your thumb and first two fingers. Tap the belly of the egg firmly against a countertop or hard, flat surface. Separate the cracked shell, and empty into a bowl.

These scrumptious breakfast egg cups are a simple but eye-catching presentation sure to impress brunch guests. These are great served with a steaming basket of Cheddar biscuits (see recipe for biscuits for Turkey Pot Pie on page 111).

BAKED EGGS WITH CHEESY POLENTA

A combination of classic cornmeal polenta and eggs with marinara, this dish comes from Italy. It makes a great supper, too, with a side of steamed broccoli or green beans.

4   cups vegetable broth or water

1   cup polenta or coarsely ground yellow cornmeal

2   cups (8 oz.) shredded Sharp Light Cheddar

¼   cup sour cream

1   cup homemade or jarred marinara sauce

12 large eggs

8   oz. Tuscan, Tomato Basil, or sharp Cheddar, cut into ⅛-inch-thick slices

¼   cup chopped basil

COAT a large (2-qt.) shallow baking dish with cooking spray, or, for individual servings, coat 6 (8- to 12-oz.) baking ramekins with cooking spray; place on a baking sheet.

BRING broth or water to a simmer in a large saucepan, and slowly whisk in cornmeal, making sure there are no lumps. Reduce heat to low, and cook, stirring continually, 15 minutes, until mixture is a very thick, smooth mass.

REMOVE polenta from heat; stir in Cheddar and sour cream until smooth. Season with salt and pepper.

PREHEAT oven to 400°. Spoon polenta into prepared baking dish, or divide evenly among individual ramekins. Top with marinara sauce, spreading evenly. Carefully break eggs on top of sauce. Season with salt and pepper. Top each egg with a slice of cheese.

BAKE 20 minutes or until eggs are cooked to your liking. Remove from oven, and let stand 5 minutes to firm up slightly. Sprinkle with basil.

MAKES 6 servings

NORTH AFRICAN SMOKY EGGS

2   Tbsp. olive oil

1   medium onion, diced

1   to 2 garlic cloves, minced

1   (14.5-oz.) can fire-roasted diced
    tomatoes, drained

½   tsp. sweet or sweet smoked paprika

¼   tsp. ground turmeric

¼   tsp. ground cumin

4   large eggs

⅔   cup (2½ oz.) shredded Garlic &
    Herb or Seriously Sharp Cheddar

HEAT oil in a medium skillet set over medium heat. Add onion to skillet, and cook, stirring occasionally, 4 to 5 minutes until softened. Add garlic and cook, stirring frequently, until fragrant.

ADD tomatoes, paprika, turmeric, and cumin to skillet; reduce heat to medium-low, and cook 5 to 7 minutes or until mixture is slightly thickened. Season with salt and pepper to taste.

WITH back of a soup spoon, make 4 slight depressions in tomato mixture; break 1 egg into each depression.

COVER skillet with lid or aluminum foil and cook until whites are just set, about 2 minutes. Break open yolks with fork to allow to spread, if desired; re-cover skillet, and cook until eggs are cooked to your liking, 1 to 2 minutes longer. Sprinkle cheese over eggs, re-cover skillet, and remove from heat. Let stand until cheese is melted, about 3 minutes. Serve hot.

MAKES 2 to 4 servings

The native name for this fragrant, slightly exotic egg dish is "shakshuka," which means "all mixed up." We like to mix it up with a few handfuls of fresh spinach or leftover cooked broccoli added to the pan with the tomatoes. Either way, it will definitely bring flavor to your morning.

TRY SOMETHING *different*

EGG AND CHEESE! Want to keep it simple? Here are some quick and tasty combos.

Bulk up the protein in your omelet by adding an egg white (or two) to one whole egg, plus a small handful of shredded Cheddar or light Cheddar. Diced leftover vegetables or a spoonful of salsa make a great filling, too.

For an omelet on-the-go, wrap up your hot cooked eggs with a little shredded cheese or cottage cheese and some fresh baby spinach in a whole wheat tortilla. Or pop them all into a pita pocket.

CHILES RELLENOS CASSEROLE

A satisfying and rib-sticking Mexican-inspired breakfast or brunch, this casserole is perfect for a hungry crowd. You can use bakery corn muffins, corn muffin mix, or if you want to bake them from scratch, see Savory Herb Corn Muffins on page 106.

12   corn muffins

6   thick slices white bread, cut into cubes

12   oz. ground turkey or pork sausage

1½   cups chopped onion

1   cup frozen corn

2   tsp. ground cumin

½   tsp. dried oregano

¼   tsp. garlic powder

3   (4-oz.) cans whole green chiles, drained and cut lengthwise into quarters

1   (15-oz.) can black beans, drained and rinsed

2   cups (8 oz.) shredded Sharp Light Cheddar, divided

4   Tbsp. butter

3   Tbsp. all-purpose flour

4   cups 2% reduced-fat milk

½   cup chopped fresh cilantro

PREHEAT oven to 350°. Crumble muffins into a large bowl. Stir in bread cubes, and set aside.

HEAT a large skillet set over medium-high heat, and add sausage and onion. Cook 5 to 7 minutes or until sausage is browned and onion is golden, stirring to break up sausage. Drain off any excess fat.

STIR in corn, cumin, oregano, and garlic powder; cook 3 to 4 minutes or until fragrant. Add sausage mixture to cornbread mixture, tossing to mix well.

COAT a 13- x 9-inch baking dish with cooking spray. Spread chiles over bottom of baking dish. Top with beans and 1 cup Cheddar. Spoon cornbread mixture evenly over cheese, and set baking dish aside.

MELT butter in a large saucepan set over medium-low heat. Whisk flour into butter, and cook 1 to 2 minutes or until golden. Gradually whisk in milk, and cook, stirring constantly, until mixture is slightly thickened and bubbling. Remove pan from heat, and stir in remaining 1 cup Cheddar. Season with salt and pepper. Pour Cheddar sauce evenly over cornbread mixture.

BAKE 25 minutes or until golden and bubbling. Let stand 10 minutes. Sprinkle with cilantro.

MAKES 10 to 12 servings

Wheeler Farm

WILMINGTON, VERMONT

ROB WHEELER TRIED LEAVING the family farm once. He went north to college for a year, but he soon came back. "I grew up always being part of the farm," he says. "It's just organic, a part of me. I couldn't wait to get back." His wife, Karen, who comes from western Massachusetts, also grew up helping out around her family's dairy farm: "It was expected if you wanted to eat dinner," she says with a smile.

Rob and his older brother John are the two of Henry and Caroline (Carrie) Wheeler's brood of seven who followed in their parents' footsteps. The farm has been in the family since 1930, and the rambling 1800s farmhouse has seen the clan grow. The other siblings and their families help out with sugaring, plowing, firewood operations, and more. Carrie, the matriarch, is still involved with the maple side of things; the Wheelers sell their own syrup and handmade maple crème candy from a roadside stand, along with vegetables like corn, pumpkin, zucchini, and tomatoes, and cut flowers from Karen's garden. "Gramp," as Rob calls his dad, still gets out to the barn daily and is full of commonsense wisdom like, "Good help always has a jackknife and a pencil."

Rob recalls that when he was young, "There were 10 of us around the table, including the hired man." His mom cooked simple, no-nonsense meals: pancakes, grilled cheese, and something called English Monkey made with eggs, bread, and lots of shredded extra sharp Cheddar served over crackers. "And always big glasses of fresh milk," Rob adds. The family milks about 60 Jerseys and a few Dutch Belted cows, with a total herd of about 120.

Karen and Rob are at the barn by 4 a.m. to milk, a chore they don't mind. "I appreciate the serenity, the peacefulness of the valley, especially in winter," she says. "You're at one with what's going on," her husband agrees. "We don't use an alarm. It just becomes your life." Between sugaring and calving, February and March are "the season of no sleep," jokes Karen, but spirits are bolstered by "the warmth of the sun melting the snow, the sight of steam rising from the sugarhouse, and the first robins."

Karen cooks for the crew members who work around the clock tending the syrup: cornbread and biscuits to be slathered with butter and hot fresh maple syrup, big pans of macaroni and cheese, and her hearty breakfast sausage bake, blueberry buckle, and sour cream coffee cakes. From milk to maple and vegetables, Rob says, "It's a very satisfying and rewarding life. It's really good to be part of a system that's feeding the world and see that more and more people are choosing to make the connection between farmers and food."

FARM FAMILY:
Henry and Carrie Wheeler with sons Rob and John

YEARS OWNED:
85 years [since 1930]

FARMSTEAD:
About 350 acres, including sugarbush

HERD:
About 120 mixed, mostly Jerseys with some Dutch Belted

OTHER FARM BUSINESS:
Maple, market garden farmstand

AWARD:
Dairy of Distinction

Karen Wheeler traditionally brings this warm, filling casserole to family breakfast gatherings at Christmas and Thanksgiving. She also makes it for the crew who've worked the overnight shift in the sugarhouse during maple season, keeping the evaporator stoked with firewood and watching the sap boil down into sweet syrup.

Wheeler Farm's
BREAKFAST SAUSAGE BAKE

4 thick slices whole grain or white bread
1 lb. ground pork sausage, browned and drained
6 large eggs
2 cups milk
1 Tbsp. yellow mustard

½ tsp. table salt
¼ tsp. freshly ground black pepper
1 cup (4 oz.) shredded Seriously Sharp Cheddar

Pure maple syrup, optional

PREHEAT oven to 350°. Coat an 11- x 7-inch baking dish with cooking spray.

TEAR bread into small pieces, and scatter over bottom of dish. Top with sausage.

WHISK eggs in a medium bowl until combined. Whisk in milk, mustard, salt, and pepper. Pour over bread and sausage. Sprinkle Cheddar over top.

BAKE, uncovered, 35 to 45 minutes or until set and a knife inserted in center comes out clean. Serve warm with maple syrup, if using.

MAKES 8 to 10 servings

TIP>> For a slightly lower-fat version that is still great tasting, substitute turkey or chicken sausage for pork.

VEGETABLE AND CHEDDAR STRATA

1	Tbsp. olive oil	1	tsp. dried thyme leaves
1	cup diced red onion	⅛	tsp. ground nutmeg
1	cup sliced mushrooms	8	cups 1-inch cubes of bakery-style whole grain bread (about 1 large loaf)
1	cup diced red bell pepper		
1	large bunch kale, washed, stems removed, and torn into pieces (about 3 cups)	1½	cups (6 oz.) shredded Seriously Sharp Cheddar
3	garlic cloves, minced	6	large eggs
		3	cups fat-free milk

COAT a 13- x 9-inch baking dish with cooking spray, and set aside.

HEAT oil in a large skillet set over medium heat. Add onion, mushrooms, and red pepper, and cook, stirring often, until soft, about 5 to 7 minutes. Add kale and cook until wilted, about 5 minutes longer. Add garlic and cook until fragrant, about 1 minute. Stir in thyme and nutmeg. Season with salt and pepper. Remove from heat, and set aside.

PLACE half the bread cubes evenly in prepared baking dish, and then top with half the vegetable mixture and half the Cheddar. Repeat layers of remaining bread cubes, vegetable mixture, and Cheddar.

WHISK eggs in a large bowl, and then whisk in milk. Season with salt and pepper. Pour egg mixture evenly over bread, vegetable mixture, and Cheddar in baking dish. Cover with aluminum foil and press down slightly to help egg mixture soak into bread. Refrigerate several hours or overnight.

WHEN ready to bake, preheat oven to 350°. Bake, uncovered, 45 to 60 minutes or until golden brown and a wooden pick inserted in center comes out clean.

MAKES 8 to 10 servings

A strata is really just an elegant name for a savory bread pudding made with eggs and cheese. This one stars a nice variety of vegetables along with some Seriously Sharp Cheddar. Note that the strata needs to sit at least several hours or overnight before baking.

Liberty Hill Farm's
GREEK-STYLE YOGURT AND FRUIT PANCAKES

These pancakes are a favorite of the guests who stay at Liberty Hill Farm (*see profile on page 74*). Beth Kennett stirs seasonal local produce like homemade applesauce, pumpkin puree, and fresh local berries into the hearty batter.

2	cups all-purpose flour	1	cup Greek-style yogurt, plain or flavored
¼	cup oat bran	1	cup applesauce or pumpkin puree
¼	cup wheat germ	½	cup butter, melted
2	Tbsp. sugar	½	cup milk
2	tsp. baking powder	2	large eggs
1	tsp. baking soda	1	cup fresh blueberries or fresh raspberries, optional
¼	tsp. table salt		

WHISK together flour, oat bran, wheat germ, sugar, baking powder, baking soda, and salt in a medium bowl; make a well in center of mixture.

WHISK together yogurt, applesauce or pumpkin puree, butter, milk, and eggs; add to dry mixture, stirring just until moistened.

POUR about ¼ cup batter for each pancake onto a hot, lightly greased griddle or large nonstick skillet. Sprinkle a few berries onto batter for each pancake, if using. Cook pancakes over medium heat 2 to 3 minutes or until tops are covered with bubbles and edges look dry and cooked; turn and cook other side.

MAKES 24 (3-inch) pancakes

KITCHEN WISDOM It's a good idea to warm your pancakes in the oven or toaster oven at 200° after you remove them from the griddle.

COTTAGE CHEESE PANCAKES

1 cup all-purpose flour	¼ tsp. table salt
¼ cup sugar	2 large eggs
1 tsp. baking powder	¾ cup cottage cheese
½ tsp. baking soda	⅔ cup milk
½ tsp. cinnamon	Maple syrup, sautéed apples, sliced bananas, or fresh berries, optional

These lightly sweet pancakes, made with cottage cheese, offer a nice change in texture and flavor from basic pancakes.

WHISK together flour, sugar, baking powder, baking soda, cinnamon, and salt in a medium bowl.

WHISK eggs in a large bowl, and then whisk in cottage cheese and milk. Stir in flour mixture just until no traces of flour remain.

PLACE a large nonstick skillet over medium heat; when hot, remove skillet from heat and coat lightly with cooking spray. Return skillet to stovetop, and add ¼ cup batter for each pancake. Cook until some of bubbles that form on surface remain open, and then flip and cook until golden on second side. Repeat with remaining batter, reducing heat to medium-low if pancakes are browning too fast.

SERVE topped with maple syrup and sautéed apples, sliced bananas, or fresh berries, if using.

MAKES about 12 (3-inch) pancakes

PROSCIUTTO AND CHEDDAR CRÊPES

2 cups seedless red grapes

2 Tbsp. olive oil

1 oz. coarsely chopped prosciutto

1½ cups baby spinach leaves

½ cup julienned (matchstick-cut) pears

⅓ cup toasted pine nuts

4 large crêpes (purchased or made from recipe below)

¾ cup (3 oz.) shredded Sharp Light Cheddar

PREHEAT oven to 350°. Combine grapes and olive oil on a rimmed baking sheet. Bake 13 to 15 minutes or until grapes begin to burst.

MEANWHILE, cook prosciutto in a large skillet until just barely crisp. Remove from heat, and cool slightly. Stir in spinach, pears, and pine nuts. Season with salt and pepper. Stir in grapes and any juices.

SPRINKLE half of one crêpe with one-fourth of the Cheddar. Top with about ¾ cup roasted grape mixture. Fold crêpe into quarters. Repeat with remaining crêpes and fillings, and serve.

MAKES 4 servings

Basic Crêpes

1 cup all-purpose flour

3 large eggs

2 Tbsp. sugar

1½ cups milk

2 Tbsp. butter, melted

WHISK together flour, eggs, and sugar in a medium bowl until well blended. Gradually whisk in milk, until batter is completely smooth. Allow batter to rest 10 minutes to 1 hour. When ready to make crêpes, heat a small to medium skillet set over medium heat. When pan is hot, lightly grease bottom and sides with melted butter (a pastry brush works well for this). Whisk crêpe batter again; with a ladle or spoon, add enough batter to cover bottom of pan very thinly. Working quickly, tilt pan so that batter coats entire bottom of pan.

AFTER about 30 seconds, when edges begin to brown and batter begins to set, flip crêpe over with a thin spatula. Cook on second side for a few seconds, and then transfer to a platter to cool. Adjust heat if crêpes are browning too slowly or quickly. Continue making crêpes until batter is all used. If stacking to refrigerate or freeze, layer with wax or parchment paper.

MAKES 12 to 16 crêpes

A sophisticated but universally appealing combination of fruit and salty Italian ham complements the nuts-and-Cheddar filling in these crêpes. You can sometimes find packaged or frozen crêpes to purchase, but they are also quite easy to make.

yogurt and fruit smoothies

It doesn't get much easier for a healthy breakfast than a smoothie with Greek-style yogurt and fruit, plus other nutritious ingredients. Combine ingredients in a blender; puree on high speed for about 45 seconds or until smooth. Adjust thickness with more liquid as desired. Serve immediately. Each recipe makes 2 servings.

SMOOTHIE	LIQUID
1 TROPICAL PARADISE	1¼ cups apricot nectar or orange juice
2 BLUEBERRY RECOVERY	1 cup bottled pure coconut water, unsweetened
3 MAPLE MOO	1 cup fat-free milk
4 NUTTY MONKEY PROTEIN	¾ cup fat-free milk
5 RASPBERRY CREAMSICLE	1 cup orange juice
6 GREEN MOUNTAIN	¾ cup apple cider or natural apple juice

YOGURT	FRUIT	OTHER INGREDIENTS
1 cup vanilla Greek-style	2 cups (about 9 oz.) frozen mango chunks	
1 cup vanilla Greek-style	2 cups frozen blueberries	
1 cup plain Greek-style	1 frozen banana, sliced (if not using frozen banana, add 1 cup ice) 1 pear, quartered	¼ cup pure maple syrup, preferably dark
1 cup plain Greek-style	2 frozen bananas, sliced (if not using frozen bananas, add 1 cup ice)	3 Tbsp. unsalted natural peanut butter 3 Tbsp. honey
1 cup vanilla Greek-style	2 cups frozen raspberries	2 Tbsp. pure maple syrup
1 cup plain Greek-style	1 frozen banana, sliced (if not using frozen banana, add 1 cup ice) 3 soft dates, pitted and halved	2 Tbsp. honey 3 cups torn kale leaves

TIP>> Smoothies make great use of overripe bananas. If you find yourself with a few extra in the fruit bowl, peel them, and cut into chunks. Freeze chunks flat on a small freezer-safe baking sheet, and then bag each banana separately so you have them premeasured and frozen when you're ready for a smoothie.

CHEESY ROASTED TOMATO AND LEEK QUICHE

There are endless ways to make your quiche just right for the occasion. This version ingeniously uses some mayonnaise to provide an extra-stable base for sweetly caramelized roasted tomatoes and leeks.

1 single piecrust, rolled out into a 9-inch pie plate and chilled (Greek-Style Yogurt Piecrust opposite page; or crust for Apple Pie with Cheddar, page 242)

6 medium-size vine-ripened tomatoes, halved and seeded

2 Tbsp. butter

2 medium leeks, white and tender green, thinly sliced

2 large eggs

¾ cup mayonnaise

¼ cup heavy cream

1½ cups (6 oz.) shredded sharp Cheddar, divided

PREHEAT oven to 375°. Line chilled piecrust with parchment paper, and fill with pie weights or uncooked rice. Bake 15 minutes. Remove parchment and pie weights, and bake until dry but not golden, another 4 to 5 minutes. Cool.

PLACE tomato halves, cut sides up, on a parchment paper–lined jelly-roll pan, and roast until just soft, about 30 minutes. Turn cut sides down and roast until tender and dry, about 20 minutes more. Cool slightly. Pinch off skins and coarsely chop.

MELT butter in a large skillet set over medium heat. Add leeks and cook, stirring occasionally, until softened and golden, about 10 to 12 minutes. Add chopped tomatoes and stir to combine, leaving big chunks of tomato.

WHISK together eggs, mayonnaise, and cream in a medium bowl. Season with salt and pepper. Stir in ½ cup Cheddar.

SCATTER ½ cup Cheddar over piecrust. Spoon leek-tomato mixture over top. Pour egg mixture over filling. Scatter with remaining ½ cup Cheddar. Bake until golden and browned in spots, about 40 minutes. Cool 10 minutes before serving.

MAKES 8 servings

TRY SOMETHING *different*

FOR OTHER FILLINGS, try feta cheese with sun-dried tomato and basil, crisp nuggets of bacon with broccoli, Canadian bacon and lightly steamed asparagus, sautéed leek and mushroom, or roasted cherry tomato and smoked turkey.

This easy, flaky piecrust uses Greek-style yogurt in place of some of the butter, and the acidity in the yogurt keeps the crust tender. The dough mixes up quickly in a bowl, requires no chilling, and rolls out easily.

Greek-Style Yogurt Piecrust

2¼ cups all-purpose flour, plus more for dusting

¼ tsp. table salt

12 Tbsp. cold butter, cut into pieces

½ cup plain Greek-style yogurt

STIR together 2¼ cups flour and salt in a large bowl. Add butter to flour mixture. Press pieces of butter with your fingertips into smaller flat flakes. Continue until you no longer feel any cold hard pieces of butter and all the butter has been flattened into ½-inch flakes.

STIR in yogurt with a fork as thoroughly as possible. (Mixture will still be totally crumbly.) Gently knead in bowl just until mixture comes together with no crumbly bits.

DIVIDE dough in half. Roll out each half between two sheets of wax paper or plastic wrap, occasionally lifting off paper or wrap from both sides to release dough from creases and allow it to spread further. (Alternatively, roll out on a lightly floured work surface.) Place in pie plate or plates as needed.

MAKES 2 (9-inch) piecrusts

CRUSTLESS SPINACH QUICHE

2 tsp. vegetable oil	1 large egg
1 medium onion, finely chopped	⅓ cup fat-free cottage cheese
1 (10-oz.) package frozen chopped spinach, thawed and drained	¼ tsp. freshly ground red pepper
1½ cups (6 oz.) shredded Sharp Light Cheddar	⅛ tsp. table salt
6 large egg whites	⅛ tsp. ground nutmeg

PREHEAT oven to 375°. Coat a 9-inch pie plate with cooking spray; set aside.

HEAT oil in a medium nonstick skillet set over medium-high heat. Add onion and cook, stirring occasionally, 5 minutes or until translucent. Add spinach and stir until moisture has evaporated, about 3 minutes.

SPRINKLE Cheddar evenly in prepared pie plate. Top with spinach mixture.

WHISK together egg whites, egg, cottage cheese, red pepper, salt, and nutmeg in a medium bowl. Pour egg mixture evenly over spinach.

BAKE 30 to 40 minutes or until set. Let stand 5 minutes, and then cut into wedges and serve.

MAKES 6 servings

For a delicious (and healthier) alternative to a standard quiche, try this crustless version, which features lots of spinach, plus light and fat-free cheeses. For more nutritional oomph, feel free to add a handful of fresh seasonal vegetables, such as sliced sautéed mushrooms or diced bell pepper.

Hot Italian Cheese Dip, page 54

Downtime

ALL-DAY NIBBLES AND NOSHES

"There are always cheese and crackers in our house. Some people have a wine refrigerator; we have one in the basement just for cheese."

—Jessica Ziehm, Tiashoke Farms, Cambridge, New York

HOT CRAB-CHEDDAR SPREAD

Add a little kick to your next gathering with this easy but elegant option served with crackers or baguette slices.

1 (8-oz.) container shredded crabmeat, drained well and checked for shell fragments

2 cups (8 oz.) shredded mild or sharp Cheddar

¼ cup mayonnaise

¼ cup plain Greek-style yogurt

¼ tsp. Worcestershire sauce

PREHEAT oven to 350°. In a medium bowl, thoroughly mix together crabmeat, Cheddar, mayonnaise, yogurt, and Worcestershire sauce. Season with salt and pepper.

SCRAPE into a small (1-qt.) baking dish. Bake 25 to 35 minutes or until lightly browned on top and bubbling at edges. Serve hot.

MAKES about 2½ cups

HOT ITALIAN CHEESE DIP

Add some Italian flair to creamy, hot cheese dip with ripe red tomatoes and fresh basil. The blend of melty Neufchâtel and Cheddar is perfect for dipping veggies, crackers, and chips.

1 (8-oz.) package Neufchâtel, softened

2 Tbsp. chopped fresh basil, divided

¼ tsp. freshly ground black pepper

Pinch of table salt

1¼ cups (5 oz.) shredded Alpine or Seriously Sharp Cheddar, divided

1 slice white bread, crusts removed, processed into fine crumbs (about ¾ cup)

½ cup chopped grape tomatoes

2 Tbsp. minced red onion

PREHEAT oven to 400°. Coat a small (about 2½-cup) ovenproof baking dish with cooking spray.

BEAT Neufchâtel in a large bowl at medium speed with an electric mixer until light and airy, about 2 minutes. Beat in 4 tsp. basil, pepper, and a pinch of salt. Add 1 cup Cheddar and breadcrumbs, and beat until blended.

SPREAD mixture in prepared dish. Top with remaining ¼ cup Cheddar. Bake 15 to 17 minutes or until heated through but not bubbling.

COOL on a wire rack about 10 minutes. Serve warm, topped with tomatoes, red onion, and remaining 2 tsp. basil.

MAKES about 2½ cups

Hot Crab-Cheddar Spread

Kenyon Hill Farm

CAMBRIDGE, NEW YORK

FARM FAMILY:
Mike and Donna
Nolan with sons, Curtis,
Shane, and Ryan

YEARS OWNED:
39 [since 1976]

FARMSTEAD:
425 owned with
another 575 rented

HERD:
About 825 Holsteins
with a few Brown Swiss,
milking 425

YOU MIGHT SAY THE KENYON HILL FARM FAMILY began at the county fair—and that event remains an annual highlight for the Nolan family. About 40 years ago, Michael Nolan met his wife, Donna, after he bought cows from her father to show at the fair. "The fair is a big deal around here," Michael says. "I remember going as a kid. It was our week's vacation every year." The couple started farming together in 1976, continuing the tradition of taking their family every August. "Late summer is fair time. We basically move over there for the week," says Curtis Nolan, the eldest of their three sons. And though their sister, Courtney, is married to another farmer, his brother Shane adds, "She still comes with us to the fair."

Donna was raised on her family's farm 18 miles away from Kenyon Hill Farm and Michael's family farmed 10 miles down road. Both knew farming was for them: "There was never a question," Michael says. "I much prefer the country life," his wife says. They moved to a new farm in 1990 and kept the name. Curtis and Shane joined their parents full time after completing college. "After I left, I became more sure of staying," Curtis says. Ryan, the youngest son, has spent several summers off-farm doing custom harvesting but has also returned for good. "It's been entirely up to them," says their father, "but in the back of your mind, you hope they will come back. It's nice to know we'll keep the farm." During the day, Donna watches the grandkids while Michael, Curtis, Shane, and Ryan manage the farm, now more than 800 head of cattle, and over 1,000 acres of cropland. ("Mom also does all the

books and takes care of all the headaches," Shane says gratefully.) They put a lot of effort into breeding, and the farm office wall is covered with beauty pageant–worthy photos of their champion cows.

The brothers gather with their wives and children for birthdays and holidays. Family get-togethers feature classics like macaroni and cheese, lasagna, roast turkey with stuffing, and Donna's famous twice-baked potato casserole with Cheddar, Parmesan, and cream cheese. "I have to make two of them now so we don't run out," she says.

Although the county fair is a unanimous favorite, there are other highlights for each family member. For Shane, it's summer "after you mow the hay on the hill and look up at it drying in windrows." For Ryan, it's the sense of accomplishment in late fall when the corn is all in. Donna also likes fall for its beautiful colors and the end of the "crazy" April through October growing and harvesting season. Her husband is alone in preferring winter. "I love the snow and snowmobiling. I just love looking at the snow. It's all quieter, calmer," Michael says. "And the kids are all home."

From left: Shane Nolan with son Graham, Curtis Nolan with sons Landon and Lucas

Kenyon Hill Farm's
CHEESY BUFFALO CHICKEN DIP

1 (8-oz.) package cream cheese or Neufchâtel, softened

⅓ cup mayonnaise

⅓ cup sour cream

⅓ cup plain Greek-style yogurt

1 tsp. fresh lemon juice

½ tsp. table salt

½ tsp. garlic powder

¼ tsp. dry mustard

½ cup hot sauce, such as Frank's Red Hot Sauce

¾ cup (3 oz.) crumbled mild blue cheese

2 large skinned and boned chicken breasts (about 1 lb.), cooked and cut into bite-size pieces

1 ½ cups (6 oz.) shredded mild Cheddar or Colby Jack

Celery sticks, carrot sticks, chips, or crackers, optional

PREHEAT oven to 350°. Spread cream cheese or Neufchâtel in bottom of a 9-inch pie plate.

WHISK together mayonnaise, sour cream, yogurt, lemon juice, salt, garlic powder, and dry mustard in a bowl until smooth. Stir in hot sauce. Stir in blue cheese and chicken.

SPREAD chicken mixture over cream cheese. Sprinkle with shredded cheese. Bake 25 minutes or until bubbly and golden. Serve hot with celery sticks, carrot sticks, chips, or crackers, if using.

MAKES 6 cups dip

The two eldest Nolan brothers, Curtis and Shane, root for different football teams, but they share a love for this indulgent dip that their mom and sister often serve on game days.

yogurt dips and toppings

Greek-style yogurt is a wonderful blank canvas for all sorts of flavors, creating an easy way to perk up simply cooked meat, seafood, or vegetables. Follow method instructions in chart. Season with salt and pepper. Use right away, or cover and refrigerate up to 3 days. Makes 1 to 2 cups.

DIP	YOGURT	SEASONINGS	OTHER INGREDIENTS
❶ GARLIC AND FETA	½ cup plain Greek-style	¼ cup chopped fresh mint 1 tsp. minced garlic	1½ cups crumbled feta cheese ½ cup sour cream
❷ BROCCOLI-CHEDDAR	⅓ cup plain Greek-style	1 tsp. minced garlic	1 cup steamed, chopped broccoli florets ¾ cup (3 oz.) shredded extra sharp Cheddar
❸ BACON & CARAMELIZED ONION	⅔ cup plain Greek-style		2 thick slices bacon, fried and crumbled ¾ cup chopped onion, slowly fried in bacon fat with 1 tsp. sugar
❹ CURRIED YOGURT	1 cup plain Greek-style	2 Tbsp. honey 1 Tbsp. curry powder 2 tsp. very finely minced or grated peeled fresh ginger	
❺ CHIPOTLE, AVOCADO, AND LIME	½ cup plain Greek-style	2 Tbsp. fresh lime juice ¼ to ½ tsp. ground chipotle pepper	2 medium avocados, mashed ¼ cup finely chopped red onion

METHOD	USES
Process	Serve with pita Top cooked veggies, seafood, chicken, lamb
Mash hot steamed, well-drained broccoli with shredded Cheddar, and then stir	Top baked potato or serve with fries Cracker spread Stir into eggs Serve with burgers, grilled chicken, or salmon
Stir	Top baked potato or roasted squash Top steamed green veggies like broccoli or green beans Spread on sandwiches
Whisk	Top baked sweet potatoes Drizzle over chicken, lamb, fish, tofu Dip for veggies
Stir	Sandwiches Dip for veggies or tortilla chips Chili topping Taco topping

TIP>> MAKING LABNEH

To make a thicker, more spreadable version of these dips, start by straining the Greek-style yogurt to extract more of the liquid. You will get something called yogurt cheese or labneh. Wrap 1 cup of plain Greek-style yogurt (2 or 10 percent) tightly in cheesecloth, and set it in a colander. Place a plate on top, and on that, a jar of water or a can to apply pressure. Leave for 12 hours in the fridge. Unwrap and scrape the yogurt cheese from the cheesecloth into a small bowl, adding whatever flavorings you like per the chart at left. Cabot chef spokesperson Jimmy Kennedy also suggests mixing in soft green herbs, lemon juice, and minced capers to serve with smoked salmon on bagel crisps; or paprika and finely diced onion to make a spread for a warm roast chicken pressed sandwich.

Pimento Cheese

TOUCHDOWN DIP

1   Tbsp. butter

1   Tbsp. all-purpose flour

¾   cup mild, medium, or hot tomato salsa

¼   cup sour cream

2   cups (8 oz.) shredded sharp Cheddar

MELT butter in a saucepan over medium heat. Add flour and stir about 30 seconds to cook flour.

STIR in salsa, and cook, stirring constantly, until mixture is simmering. Stir in sour cream.

ADD Cheddar and continue stirring until cheese is completely melted and mixture returns to a simmer.

TRANSFER to a serving bowl, and serve hot.

MAKES about 2 cups

Score major points with this take on chile con queso. Bottled salsa makes prep simple, and adding a little flour keeps it smooth and creamy. Serve it hot with tortilla chips and veggies.

PIMENTO CHEESE

1   cup (4 oz.) shredded Seriously Sharp Cheddar

1   cup (4 oz.) shredded Sharp Light Cheddar

2   Tbsp. plain Greek-style yogurt

2   Tbsp. reduced-fat mayonnaise

1   (4-oz.) jar chopped pimentos, drained well

Dash of hot sauce, such as Tabasco

Celery sticks, crackers, or toast triangles, optional

COMBINE sharp Cheddar, light Cheddar, yogurt, mayonnaise, pimentos, and hot sauce in a medium bowl. Season with salt. Refrigerate until ready to serve. Serve on celery sticks, spread on crackers, or broiled on toast triangles, if using.

MAKES 1¼ cups

Freund's Farm's THREE CHEESE LOG

1 cup (4 oz.) shredded sharp Cheddar

¼ cup chopped drained jarred roasted red bell peppers

2 Tbsp. thinly sliced fresh chives

½ tsp. dry mustard

1½ tsp. Worcestershire sauce

4 oz. cream cheese or Neufchâtel, softened

¼ cup (1 oz.) crumbled blue cheese

½ cup finely chopped toasted walnuts or pecans, or a combination

Apple, pear, or bread slices, pickled onions, and crackers, optional

COMBINE Cheddar, peppers, chives, dry mustard, Worcestershire sauce, cream cheese or Neufchâtel, and blue cheese in the bowl of an electric mixer. Beat at medium speed until blended.

PLACE a 10-inch square piece of plastic wrap on work surface. Sprinkle nuts in center of plastic wrap.

WITH moist hands, shape cheese mixture into an 8-inch log. Place log on nuts, rolling to coat. Roll up log in plastic wrap, twisting ends to seal. Chill at least 2 hours.

SERVE with apple, pear, or bread slices, pickled onions, and crackers, if using.

MAKES 1 log (about 2½ cups spread)

TRY SOMETHING *different*

FRUIT AND CHEDDAR APPETIZERS Fruit and Cheddar pair beautifully. Here are a few quick, elegant appetizer ideas.

Bacon-Wrapped Pears with Horseradish Cheddar: Wrap lemon juice–brushed pear wedges and thinly shaved Horseradish Cheddar with hot, cooked (but still pliable) bacon. Skewer with a wooden pick and serve.

Cheddar-Chutney Stuffed Apricots: Mix together 1 cup shredded extra sharp Cheddar with ½ cup sweetened dried cranberries and 2 Tbsp. chutney. Stuff into dried apricots, and press chopped pistachios onto exposed filling.

Apple, Cheddar, and Walnut Toasts: Broil toasted baguette rounds topped with sliced apple and grated Horseradish Cheddar and a walnut half.

Cheddar with Honey, Walnuts, and Dried Cherries: Place block of Cheddar on a serving board or plate; sprinkle with chopped, toasted walnuts and chopped dried cherries or figs; and drizzle with honey.

YOGURT CURRY DEVILED EGGS

6   large eggs
1   tsp. honey
1   tsp. yellow mustard
½   tsp. curry powder
½   tsp. cider vinegar

⅛   tsp. ground red pepper
About ½ cup 2% reduced-fat plain
     Greek-style yogurt
¼   cup finely sliced green onions
     and/or shredded carrot, optional

PLACE eggs in a single layer in a stainless steel saucepan (do not use nonstick). Add water to a depth of 3 inches. Bring to a rolling boil; cover, remove from heat, and let stand 15 minutes. Drain immediately, and return eggs to pan. Fill pan with cold water and ice. Cover pan and shake vigorously to crack eggs all over.

PEEL eggs, cut lengthwise, and remove yolks to a small bowl.

ADD honey, mustard, curry powder, vinegar, and pepper to bowl; mash together with back of a spoon until no lumps remain. Whisk in enough yogurt for desired consistency. Salt to taste.

FILL each egg-white half with yolk mixture. Garnish with green onions, carrot, or both, if using.

MAKES 12 deviled egg halves

Everyone loves a good deviled egg, and Greek-style yogurt gives them a delicious tang, along with a lighter flavor.

the perfect cheese plate

Offering a cheese plate for a gathering can be both a fun way to break the ice and explore the flavors and textures of different cheeses. Start with mild ones, and then sample the stronger flavored cheeses.

TYPE OF CHEESE

1 FRESH AND MILD CHEESE
(chèvre, ricotta, mozzarella)

Very mild-tasting and usually not too rich

2 BLOOMY RIND, CAMEMBERT-STYLE CHEESE
(usually cow, but could be sheep or a blend) and double or triple crèmes

Mild and creamy

> You can eat the white rind, if you like.

3 SEMI-SOFT TO SEMI-FIRM CHEESES
such as medium to sharp Cheddar, Monterey Jack, semi-aged sheep and goat cheeses

Growing strength of flavors and firmer textures

4 BOLDLY FLAVORED HARD CHEESES
like more mature (longer-aged) Cheddar, Swiss, or milder washed-rind cheese

5 CHEESE WITH DOMINANT PRESENCE
such as stinky washed-rind and big blues

Powerful smell and lasting flavor

SUGGESTED ACCOMPANIMENTS	BEVERAGE PAIRINGS
Fresh tomatoes, mint, or basil to match freshness Good olive oil or honey to balance usually salty flavor	Light or fruity beverages that complement fresh flavors: blonde and pale ales like Saison, crisp white wines or light reds like gamay-based Beaujolais, chilled green tea
Apples, pears, berries complement mildness with soft fruitiness. Maple or honey-glazed nuts Acidity of sun-dried tomatoes cuts the cream. Sweet flavor and crunchy texture of dried fruit and nut breads or crackers pair well with mild, smooth-textured double and triple crèmes.	Fruit-infused beer such as framboise; a light and dry hard cider; off-dry champagne-style wine; sour beer to cut creaminess with acidity and underline mildness with light fruity notes; citrus-infused seltzer
Pickled vegetables complement tanginess of aged goat and sheep cheeses. Acidity of green or other tart apples go well with Cheddars and aged Monterey Jack.	Medium-weight beers like pilsner or amber lagers; medium-bodied wines such as pinot blanc and lighter fruity reds such as pinot noir or zinfandel; dry hard cider
The rich flavors of cranberry or apple chutneys pair well with aged Cheddar. The sweet flavor and thick texture of long-aged balsamic vinegar pair well with the sweet, nutty flavor of aged Parmesan. The salt and fat in cured meats match well with the hard, drier cheeses.	Pale ales and other more hoppy beers with some backbone to stand up to the cheeses; wines with more heft like oaky chardonnay or fruity cabernet sauvignon with soft tannins; hard ciders on the crisp and dry side or fresh nonalcoholic apple cider that is not too sweet
The earthy flavors of mushrooms and blue cheese pair well. Rich, sweet dried fruits and dark chocolate	Stout and dopplebock beers; big, bold cabernet sauvignons; and dessert wines such as Sauternes and Port

Round out the platter
Include some bread or crackers and sliced apples or pears, grapes, nuts, chutneys, or preserves like this simple tomato jam, which is a perfect complement to Cheddar.

SIMPLE TOMATO JAM
Mix together in a small saucepan, and simmer over medium-low heat until thick:

2 cups diced ripe Roma tomatoes + ¼ cup packed light brown sugar + 1½ Tbsp. fresh lime juice + 2 tsp. minced fresh ginger + ¼ tsp. ground chipotle pepper + ⅛ tsp. table salt

TIP>> FOCUS ON THREE TO FIVE cheeses representing three of the general categories outlined at left; too many choices can be overwhelming.

PRESENT A VARIETY of milk—cow, sheep, goat—or, if you prefer, stick with one kind of milk and contrast styles of cheese instead.

BRING ALL CHEESES to room temperature before serving.

MAKE TAGS for each cheese so guests know what they're tasting.

SUGGEST AN ORDER in which to taste: from lighter to stronger flavors.

CHEDDAR FLATBREAD

This toasty, cheesy flatbread is great by itself as a snack, cut into triangles with any of our dips, or as a perfect accompaniment to soup and salad.

1½ cups warm water (110° to 115°)

2 tsp. sugar

1 (¼-oz.) envelope active dry yeast

3¼ to 3½ cups all-purpose flour

2 Tbsp. extra virgin olive oil, plus more for rising and cooking

2 tsp. table salt

2 cups (8 oz.) shredded extra sharp or sharp Cheddar

COMBINE warm water and sugar in bowl of an electric stand mixer. Stir until sugar is dissolved, and then sprinkle yeast on top. Let stand until yeast is dissolved and foamy, about 10 minutes.

ADD 3¼ cups of flour, oil, and salt, and knead mixture with dough hook on medium speed 5 minutes until smooth and elastic, adding more flour as needed if dough doesn't come cleanly away from sides of bowl. (It will still be slightly sticky.)

ADD cheese and knead about 1 minute longer or until well mixed. (Alternatively, make dough in food processor, kneading in cheese by hand at end, or make entirely by hand, kneading for 8 to 10 minutes.)

PLACE dough in an oiled bowl, turning to coat, cover with plastic wrap, and set aside to rise until doubled in volume, 1 to 2 hours. (If you don't wish to use all of dough immediately, you may wrap it well and refrigerate up to 2 days or freeze up to 3 months; bring back to room temperature before shaping and baking.)

PREHEAT grill to medium-high or oven to 450°, ideally with a pizza stone. Punch down dough, and divide into 4 equal pieces. Stretch or lightly roll each piece into an approximate 10-inch round. Brush top of each round with a little more oil.

IF USING GRILL, place rounds, oiled sides down, on grill, and cook until browned on underside, 2 to 4 minutes. Brush tops with additional oil, turn rounds over with tongs, and cook until browned on second side and cooked through to center, 1 to 2 minutes longer. If using oven, place rounds, oiled sides down, on pizza stone or baking sheet, and brush top with additional oil. Bake 5 to 6 minutes, and then turn rounds over with tongs, and bake another 2 to 3 minutes until golden.

REMOVE to cutting board. Top as desired, or cut into pieces and serve.

MAKES 4 (10-inch) flatbreads

TIP>> JUST AFTER YOU PULL THE CHEDDAR FLAT-BREAD OUT OF THE OVEN, embellish it with caramelized onions, a scattering of slivered salami, and sliced marinated artichoke hearts; or try chopped steamed shrimp, arugula, and diced sun-dried tomatoes in oil.

YOU CAN ALSO MAKE KID-FRIENDLY PIZZA BITES: Just cut out 3- to 4-inch circles of dough, fill with a scant tablespoon of marinara sauce and diced pepperoni or cooked vegetables, moisten the edge of the dough with water, and seal shut into half-moon shapes before baking 5 to 7 minutes or until golden.

BEAN-CHEESE SPIRALS

These 3-step snacks are a super-easy way to add variety to a party appetizer spread or provide a protein-rich after-school bite for the kids.

1	(15-oz.) can black beans, drained and rinsed	2	rectangular sheets soft whole wheat lavash bread or other wrap
2	Tbsp. olive oil	1	cup (4 oz.) shredded chipotle, sharp, or extra sharp Cheddar
1	Tbsp. fresh lime juice		Tomato salsa to serve, optional
2	tsp. ground cumin		

MASH beans, oil, lime juice, and cumin coarsely with a potato masher or fork in a medium bowl. Season with salt and pepper.

SPREAD half of mixture over each lavash or other wrap. Sprinkle with cheese. Starting with wide side, roll up tightly.

WRAP in plastic wrap, and refrigerate until ready to serve. Cut off 1-inch slices. Place, cut sides down, on a microwave-safe plate, and microwave at HIGH just until warm, about 20 seconds for 4 spirals. (Alternatively, heat in toaster oven or oven at 350° about 5 minutes or until warmed through.) Serve with tomato salsa for dipping, if using.

MAKES 24 spirals

PEPPER JACK–ARTICHOKE HUMMUS

1 (15-oz.) can chickpeas,
   drained and rinsed

1 ½ cups (6 oz.) shredded Pepper Jack

2 Tbsp. fresh lemon juice

½ tsp. ground cumin

¼ tsp. table salt

1 (14-oz.) can artichoke hearts, drained

COMBINE chickpeas, Pepper Jack, lemon juice, cumin, and salt in food processor bowl, and process 2 to 3 minutes, or until very smooth, scraping down sides of bowl as needed.

FIRMLY squeeze liquid out of each artichoke heart, 1 at a time, and add to processor bowl. Pulse until hearts are finely chopped but not pureed.

SERVE immediately, or refrigerate until serving. Let stand at room temperature to soften if hummus has been refrigerated.

MAKES about 2½ cups

Pepper Jack adds both heat and creamy texture to this simple appetizer. Serve with crackers, crisps, and fresh vegetables.

TRY SOMETHING *different*

MORE SNACK-TASTIC SUGGESTIONS...

Nutty Carrot Balls: Mash together 4 oz. Neufchâtel with 1 cup shredded Cheddar and ¼ cup grated carrots; with moistened hands, roll into 1-inch balls, and coat in chopped roasted sunflower seeds or nuts, if desired.

Lettuce Rollups: Mound a tablespoon each of shredded turkey breast, shredded Cheddar, and grated carrot or halved grapes in a soft lettuce leaf, and roll up.

Pear or Apple Boats: Mix together shredded Cheddar and raisins or dried cranberries with a little mayonnaise or vanilla or plain Greek-style yogurt. Seed and halve pears or apples, and then fill with cheese-and-fruit mixture.

Warm Cheese Dunk: Whisk together ¼ cup milk and 1 tsp. cornstarch until cornstarch is dissolved. Microwave or bring to a boil, stirring, until thickened. Take off heat, and stir in 1 cup shredded mild Cheddar or Monterey Jack. Serve with veggies and whole wheat pretzels.

NESTLED BETWEEN LIBERTY HILL AND JERUSALEM HILL, appropriately near the Delectable Mountains, sits Beth and Bob Kennett's Liberty Hill Farm. In addition to milking about 110 cows, raising their own replacement milkers, and breeding prime bulls for sale, Beth and Bob welcome overnight guests for farmstays, which they have done for 30 years. Guests get a behind-the-scenes look into the rhythms of daily farming life, hike and snowshoe around the property, and are treated to bountiful and yes, delectable, farm-fresh morning and evening meals. "We have made the most phenomenal friendships," Beth says, some of which, she adds, now span generations. "The world has come to us."

Farming roots run deep in the family, and Liberty Hill Farm itself dates back to the 1780s; one corner of the majestic five-story barn, topped by a cow-shaped weather vane, is 225 years old. The Kennetts, who today work the farm with their two grown sons, Tom and David, actually first spied the farm when they were on their honeymoon nearby and set their hearts on it. Not until a few years later did it come up for sale and, serendipitously, they happened to be in the right place at the right time. "We said, 'That's our farm,'" Beth recalls, "and wrote a check for $500—all the money we had."

The big, open kitchen is the heart of the farm, where Beth bakes, cooks, and serves up elegant Cheddar puffs, classic biscuit-topped Vermont chicken pie, and magically

Liberty Hill Farm
ROCHESTER, VERMONT

fudgy chocolate cake made with Greek-style yogurt. "I started making apple pies when I was nine," Beth says. "My grandmother was my inspiration. She cooked out of love, from the heart. My grandparents had a huge garden, and what they didn't eat, they put up. And whatever they didn't have room for, they gave to neighbors."

As David's toddler daughter, Ella, sits at her grandparents' kitchen table poring over photos of cows in the latest issue of *Holstein International,* Beth notes that her son showed the same fascination with cows from an early age. "We call him the cow whisperer," Beth says. "Since he was 4, he's churned out cow statistics like other kids know sports statistics." The Kennetts were careful not to pressure their boys into farming, urging them to go to college and pursue other interests. "We always felt very strongly that they needed to choose farming," Beth explains. "It's 24/7/365. When you're a famer, it's your identity, it's your life. It's not 9 to 5 and you clock out. It's who you are."

That said, it was a huge relief when both sons came home to farm and developed complementary areas of expertise: David in genetics and breeding; Tom in fieldwork. But Beth acknowledges, "Our farm probably wouldn't survive if our sons hadn't come home to farm with us. It's a blessing."

AWARDS:
Dairy of Distinction; 2013 Vermont Innkeeper of the Year; *Yankee Magazine* Editor's Choice Best of New England; Vermont's first certified Green Agritourism Enterprise; Bob Kennett has received the Holstein Assocation of America's Progressive Breeders Registry Award annually for more than 20 years.

Liberty Hill Farm's
VERMONT CHEDDAR PUFFS

Beth Kennett has fond memories of her grandmother's cream puffs. These puffs, also known as gougères, are the savory equivalent. They look fancy but are very easy, Beth promises (and a good workout for your arms). The cheese puffs can be filled with a mixture of softened cream cheese and sour cream blended with smoked salmon and chives.

1   cup all-purpose flour

1   tsp. dry mustard

Pinch of ground red pepper

½   cup butter, cut into cubes

¼   tsp. table salt

¼   tsp. sugar

4   large eggs

1½   cups (6 oz.) sharp Cheddar, extra sharp Cheddar, Seriously Sharp Cheddar, or Private Stock Cheddar

⅓   cup (1⅓ oz.) grated Parmesan cheese, divided

PREHEAT oven to 425°. Line two baking sheets with parchment paper or silicone baking mats. Whisk together flour, dry mustard, and red pepper in a small bowl, and set aside.

HEAT 1 cup water, butter, salt, and sugar in a medium saucepan set over medium-high heat until butter is melted and mixture is just coming to a boil.

ADD flour mixture all at once, and stir vigorously with a wooden spoon until mixture breaks away from side of pan and forms a smooth ball.

REMOVE saucepan from heat, and let rest 2 minutes. Beat in eggs, 1 at a time, stirring quickly, so egg doesn't cook, and making sure each egg is fully incorporated before adding the next, until dough is firm and smooth.

STIR in Cheddar and all but 2 Tbsp. of Parmesan until well blended.

TRANSFER mixture to a pastry bag fitted with large plain tip. Pipe dough into 24 small round mounds, about 1 inch apart. (Alternately, use two teaspoons to form and drop tablespoonfuls of batter onto baking sheets.) Sprinkle tops with remaining 2 Tbsp. Parmesan.

BAKE 10 minutes. Reduce oven temperature to 375°, and bake 18 to 20 minutes longer or until evenly golden brown. Cool on racks or serve hot.

MAKES 24 cheese puffs

HOT AS A TORCH! JALAPEÑO POPPERS

12 jalapeño peppers, about 2½ inches long

1 cup (4 oz.) mild Cheddar or sharp Cheddar

3 oz. cream cheese or Neufchâtel, softened

¼ tsp. garlic powder

¼ tsp. ground chipotle pepper or chili powder

2 large eggs

⅔ cup fine, dry breadcrumbs

½ tsp. table salt

Sour cream to serve, optional

PREHEAT oven to 325°. Lightly oil a baking sheet, and set aside. Cut peppers in half lengthwise; scrape out and discard seeds. (Take care when working with hot peppers: Don't touch your eyes until you've washed your hands very well.)

MIX together Cheddar, cream cheese or Neufchâtel, garlic powder, and chipotle pepper or chili powder in a small bowl. Fill each pepper with mixture.

LIGHTLY beat eggs in a shallow bowl or pie plate until combined and frothy. Stir together breadcrumbs and salt in another shallow bowl. Roll each filled pepper in egg, and then in breadcrumbs. Place on prepared baking sheet.

BAKE until tender and browned, about 30 minutes. Serve warm, with sour cream for dipping, if using.

MAKES 24 jalapeño poppers

These simple but spicy baked jalapeño poppers make the perfect appetizer for your next party or the big game. You can make them ahead of time, and if you'd like, use Chipotle or Hot Habanero Cheddar and skip the chipotle or chili powder.

CHEDDAR CHEESE STRAWS

½ cup cold water

1⅓ cups all-purpose flour, plus more
for dusting

Pinch of freshly ground red pepper

Pinch of table salt

½ cup cold butter, cut into cubes

1½ cups (6 oz.) shredded sharp or
extra sharp Cheddar, divided

Buttery and savory, these elegant straws can also be rolled and cut into all sorts of shapes. Whatever their shape, they are addictive!

PLACE several ice cubes in a small bowl or cup, and add about ½ cup cold water; set aside to chill. Preheat oven to 400°. Generously butter two baking sheets, or coat with nonstick cooking spray.

PULSE flour, red pepper, and salt together in the bowl of a food processor. Add butter to flour mixture, and pulse about 10 times until butter is no more than the size of peas. (Alternatively, whisk flour, red pepper, and salt together in bowl, and then work in butter with fingertips.)

ADD 1 cup of Cheddar, and pulse several times to blend. Pulse in just enough ice water, 1 tablespoon at a time, to make a dough that is crumbly but holds together when firmly squeezed. (Alternatively, use a fork to stir in Cheddar, and then stir in ice water, a tablespoon at a time, to mixture in bowl.) Turn mixture onto work surface, and press into a rough square.

DUSTING dough and work surface lightly with flour as needed, roll dough out into an approximate 12-inch square. Sprinkle one half of square with remaining ½ cup Cheddar. Fold bare half of dough over Cheddar. Neaten edge of rectangle roll into a 20-inch-long strip about 8 inches wide.

WITH knife or pastry wheel, cut strip crosswise into ½-inch-wide straws. Place about ½ inch apart on prepared baking sheets.

BAKE 8 to 12 minutes or until golden brown, watching carefully toward end of baking time. Remove from baking sheets, and cool on a wire rack.

MAKES about 3 dozen

APPLE-CHEDDAR MINI PHYLLO QUICHES

Paper-thin and delicate layered phyllo (filo) pastry shells are available these days at your local grocery, so whipping up fancy hors d'oeuvres is easy.

45 mini frozen phyllo pastry shells, thawed according to package instructions

1 large crisp, sweet-tart apple, such as McIntosh, finely diced

4 large eggs

2 Tbsp. half-and-half

½ tsp. table salt

¼ tsp. white pepper

¼ tsp. ground nutmeg

1 ½ cups (6 oz.) shredded Farmhouse Reserve or extra sharp Cheddar

PREHEAT oven to 350°. Line a baking sheet with parchment paper or aluminum foil. Lay phyllo shells out on prepared baking sheet. Divide apple evenly among cups.

BEAT eggs with half-and-half, salt, pepper, and nutmeg. Transfer to a glass measuring cup. Pour carefully into phyllo cups, dividing evenly. Top each with about 1½ tsp. Cheddar.

CAREFULLY transfer to the oven, and bake 15 to 17 minutes or until filling is puffed and golden. Cool at least 3 minutes before serving.

MAKES 45 bite-size appetizers

TRY SOMETHING *different*

A CLASSIC PAIRING... Here are some specific varieties of apple that taste just right with certain types of Cheddar.

APPLE VARIETY	CHEDDAR	HOW TO PAIR
GALA: mild, sweet, juicy	Extra sharp	Caramelize peeled, diced apple with a little butter, light brown sugar, and golden raisins. Top a cracker with sliced Cheddar and a spoonful of warm apple chutney.
MCINTOSH: sweet with a tart edge, extra juicy	Seriously Sharp	Mix shredded Cheddar with dried cranberries, chopped pecans, and plain Greek-style yogurt to moisten. Dollop on cored rounds of apple.
BRAEBURN: rich, spicy-sweet, crisp, juicy	Habanero	Toss shredded Cheddar with arugula, thinly sliced apple, and crumbled bacon with a light cider vinegar dressing.
GRANNY SMITH: tart, juicy	Pepper Jack	Sandwich grated pepper Jack with thinly sliced apple and smoked turkey between whole wheat tortillas, cook on the griddle until melted, and cut in triangles.
GOLDEN DELICIOUS: very sweet, juicy	Garlic & Herb	Broil up mini "pitzas" with whole wheat pita pockets topped with sliced apple, a little honey mustard, and shredded Cheddar.

TIP>> For a different flavor combo, try a pear instead.

Chicken and
Corn Tortilla Soup,
page 88

In From the Cold

SOUPS, CHILIS, AND STEWS

"When we first took in guests on the farm, my neighbor said to me, 'Don't make anything too fancy. Serve them real Vermont cooking done well,' and she taught me how to make a Vermont chicken pot pie with biscuits on top."

—Beth Kennett, Liberty Hill Farm,
Rochester, Vermont

BROCCOLI-CHEDDAR SOUP

Chunky and savory, this simple soup is quick to whip up for a weeknight supper served with good bread and a crunchy slaw or salad like the Bulgur, Cucumber, and Chickpea Salad on page 207.

2 Tbsp. butter

2 cups peeled and diced boiling potatoes (about 2 medium)

½ cup chopped onion

2 Tbsp. all-purpose flour

2 cups milk

1 (14-oz.) can chicken or vegetable broth (1¾ cups)

3 cups broccoli (chopped florets and thinly sliced stems)

2 cups (8 oz.) shredded sharp Cheddar or extra sharp Cheddar

1 tsp. fresh lemon juice

MELT butter in a large saucepan set over medium heat. Add potatoes and onion, and cook, stirring occasionally, until onion is tender, about 5 minutes. Add flour and cook, stirring constantly, 2 minutes.

GRADUALLY stir in milk and broth. Bring to a simmer, and cook until potatoes are nearly tender, about 5 minutes. Add broccoli and cook until broccoli is tender, about 5 minutes longer.

REMOVE from heat, and stir in Cheddar. Add lemon juice, and season with salt and pepper.

MAKES 4 servings

CREAMY CHEESY CAULIFLOWER SOUP

1 cup chopped onion	½ cup fat-free milk
1 medium head (about 1½ lb.) cauliflower, roughly chopped	½ cup (2 oz.) shredded Sharp Light Cheddar
2½ cups reduced-sodium chicken or vegetable broth	2 Tbsp. chopped fresh dill

COAT a large saucepan with cooking spray, and place over medium heat. Add onion and sauté until tender, about 3 minutes. Add cauliflower and cook 2 minutes.

ADD broth and milk to pan; bring to a boil. Reduce heat and simmer, covered, 30 minutes or until cauliflower is very tender.

REMOVE from heat; puree soup in a blender or food processor in batches. (Alternatively, puree with an immersion blender.)

RETURN soup to pan set over medium-low heat. Whisk in Cheddar, and cook, stirring constantly, just until cheese melts. Season with salt and pepper, sprinkle with dill, and serve.

MAKES 4 servings

In our deceptively rich-tasting soup, cauliflower delivers smoothness without the cream.

KITCHEN WISDOM Use great care when blending hot liquids like soup. Leave the center of the blender lid off or the feed tube of the food processor open, and cover the opening with a wadded kitchen towel to prevent dangerous steam buildup. Always start slowly, and don't overfill your machine, blending soup in batches, if necessary.

CHICKEN AND CORN TORTILLA SOUP

With punchy flavor and great textures, this quick and light soup makes a great meal paired with our Savory Herb Corn Muffins (see page 106).

1 ½ lb. skinned and boned chicken breasts

1   Tbsp. vegetable oil

½   cup chopped onion

2   cloves garlic, minced

4   cups reduced-sodium chicken broth

1   lb. fresh or frozen corn kernels

1   (10-oz.) can diced tomatoes and green chiles, undrained

Corn tortilla chips, shredded Sharp Light Cheddar, diced avocado, and plain Greek-style yogurt to serve

PLACE chicken breasts and 4 cups water in a large saucepan set over medium-high heat. Bring to a simmer, skim off any foam, reduce heat to maintain a gentle simmer, and cover. Cook just until chicken is cooked through, about 8 to 10 minutes. Transfer chicken to a plate to cool. Reserve cooking liquid.

HEAT oil in a large soup pot set over medium-high heat. Add onion and cook, stirring frequently, until tender, about 3 to 4 minutes. Add garlic and cook, stirring often, until fragrant, about 1 minute.

ADD chicken broth and 2 cups reserved cooking liquid to soup pot, and bring to a simmer. Add corn and cook 5 minutes. Add tomatoes and green chiles and cooked chicken; cook 5 minutes or until heated through. Add more reserved cooking liquid, if desired. Season with salt and pepper.

LADLE soup into bowls over tortilla chips, and top with shredded light Cheddar, avocado, and dollops of yogurt, if using.

MAKES 6 to 8 servings

TOMATO-CHEDDAR SOUP

2   Tbsp. olive oil

1   cup chopped yellow onion

2   tsp. minced garlic

2   Tbsp. all-purpose flour

1   (28-oz.) can Italian plum tomatoes, undrained

1   (14-oz.) can chicken broth (1¾ cups)

½   cup half-and-half or milk

3   sprigs fresh thyme or ½ tsp. dried thyme leaves

2   cups (8 oz.) shredded sharp Cheddar or extra sharp Cheddar, plus extra for garnish

Croutons, optional

HEAT oil in a large pot set over medium heat. Add onion and cook, stirring often, until soft and translucent, about 5 minutes. Add garlic and cook, stirring frequently, 30 seconds. Add flour; cook, stirring constantly, 1 minute.

REMOVE pan from heat. Add tomatoes, crushing each into smaller pieces with your hand as you add them. Pour in remaining liquid from tomatoes, and stir until well combined with onion mixture. Add broth, half-and-half or milk, and thyme; stir together well.

RETURN pot to medium-high heat, and bring mixture to a boil. Adjust heat to maintain a simmer; cover pot, and cook 15 minutes, stirring occasionally to be sure nothing is sticking to bottom of pot.

REMOVE from heat. Remove and discard thyme sprigs. Add Cheddar a handful at a time, stirring until cheese is melted.

PUREE soup in a blender in batches until smooth (see tip on page 87). (Alternatively, puree with an immersion blender.) Return soup to pot. Season with salt and pepper.

PLACE over medium heat, and cook, stirring occasionally, just until heated through. Serve topped with croutons and additional shredded Cheddar, if using.

MAKES 6 servings

What could be better than tomato soup and grilled cheese? Melting some tangy sharp Cheddar into the soup, of course.

Another favorite, our creamy Cheddar-Ale Soup, balances rich Cheddar with the bite of Irish red ale, but almost any robust beer will work. (Just avoid anything too hoppy, as it can cook down with a bitter edge.)

CHEDDAR-ALE SOUP

4 Tbsp. butter	2½ cups 1% low-fat milk
½ cup minced onion	1 (14-oz.) can chicken broth (1¾ cups)
¼ cup minced carrot	1 tsp. dry mustard
¼ cup minced celery	4 cups (1 lb.) shredded sharp Cheddar, extra sharp Cheddar, or Seriously Sharp Cheddar
1 small bay leaf	
⅓ cup all-purpose flour	3 strips bacon, cooked and crumbled, optional
1 (12-oz.) bottle Irish red ale	

MELT butter in a large saucepan set over medium heat. Add onion, carrot, celery, and bay leaf, and cook, stirring often, until vegetables are translucent and softened, about 4 minutes. Stir in flour and cook, stirring often, about 3 minutes. Gradually whisk in ale, stirring frequently, about 2 minutes or until mixture is bubbling and thickened. Whisk in milk, chicken broth, and dry mustard. Bring soup to a simmer, stirring often.

ADD Cheddar a handful at a time; stir until cheese is melted and soup is hot, but do not let soup boil. Remove pan from heat; discard bay leaf. Season with salt and pepper. Garnish with bacon, if using.

MAKES 6 servings

SWEET POTATO–CHEDDAR SOUP WITH CHIPOTLE

3   Tbsp. olive oil

1   cup diced onion

1   cup chopped celery

¾   tsp. table salt

1   tsp. ground cumin

¼   tsp. ground cinnamon

2   large sweet potatoes (about 1 lb. each), peeled and cut into 1 ½-inch chunks

6   cups reduced-sodium chicken or vegetable broth

1   canned chipotle pepper in adobo sauce, minced, or more to taste (see tip below)

2   Tbsp. apple cider vinegar

1½   cups (6 oz.) shredded Farmhouse Reserve Cheddar or extra sharp Cheddar

2   sliced green onions for garnish, optional

HEAT oil in a large heavy-bottomed pot set over medium-high heat. Add onion, celery, and salt, and cook, stirring occasionally, until onion is softened and starting to brown, about 7 minutes.

STIR in cumin and cinnamon, and cook just until spices are fragrant, about 30 seconds. Add sweet potatoes and broth; cover pot, increase heat to high, and bring to a simmer.

REDUCE heat to medium-low to maintain a gentle simmer and cook, uncovered, until potatoes are completely soft and falling apart, about 20 minutes. Add chipotle pepper and vinegar, and remove from heat.

PUREE soup in a blender in batches until smooth (see tip on page 87). (Alternatively, puree with an immersion blender.)

RETURN soup to pot, and warm over medium heat. Add Cheddar, stirring just until cheese is completely melted. Season with salt and pepper. Garnish with green onions, if using.

MAKES 6 servings

TIP>> If you don't have canned chipotles on hand, use chipotle chile powder, starting off with ¼ tsp. and adding more to taste.

Warm up your next meal with a bowl of this nourishing sweet potato soup spiced up with a little chipotle pepper in adobo sauce.

Barstow's
Longview Farm

HADLEY, MASSACHUSETTS

"THERE'S A LOT OF US BARSTOWS," Marjorie says with a smile. She pulls a batch of crisp, golden cookies from the oven. No timer needed: "I just know when they're ready," the 93-year-old matriarch says. She enjoyed raising her family of five on the farm, and she is proud of the fact that she threw hay bales along with the men. Marjorie recognizes the farming life is not for everyone, but love of the land and animals runs deep in the family. Barstows have farmed this land in the Pioneer Valley of western Massachusetts since 1806. Her late husband, Nelson, "loved this farm, and he stayed active up till the end." Marjorie reflects quietly. "The day he died, he made his own sandwich right here."

Their grandson Steve has always felt that same connection. "When we were kids, if Steve misbehaved, he wasn't allowed to go to the farm," his sister Kelly says. "That was the only consequence he cared about." Steve is working with his dad and uncle to transition into a leadership role with the 450-cow herd and about 400 acres of cropland. "I think waking up every day and seeing all this here motivates me," he says, gesturing to the barns, fields, and the family homes on the property.

Kelly, on the other hand, had no intention of going into the family business. "When I was a teenager, I wanted to do anything but," she says with a smile. But after studying and working out of state for several years, she came home to help with the store and the finances, as well as coordinate the farm's busy schedule of school tours for grade-schoolers to university students majoring in animal science and biotechnology. The farm works hard on reducing its environmental footprint with a composting operation and a recently completed methane digester that produces enough electricity to power 250 houses; the dairy herd even chows down on piles of potato seconds from a local vegetable farm. "I really like working toward something that's helping my family sustain this land and our community," Kelly says.

Their younger sister Shannon, in turn, dreamed of having a bakery since she was 13, which was a big factor in the family's decision to open their on-farm dairy store and bakery in 2008. Shannon learned to bake from her grandmother and was a natural, as Marjorie proudly notes, winning a blue ribbon at the fair shortly after she first mastered pie crust. Shannon's team also makes from-scratch soups and stews like corn and Cheddar chowder, chili with the farm's own beef, and quiches. It remains to be seen whether customers will ever get to taste Grandma Barstow's legendary cinnamon buns, however; so far Marjorie has not been willing to share that recipe.

FARM FAMILY:
Marjorie Barstow and her sons David and Steve and grandchildren, Steven II, Kelly, and Shannon

YEARS OWNED:
209 [since 1806]

FARMSTEAD:
About 400 acres

HERD:
450 Holsteins

OTHER FARM BUSINESS:
Farm store and bakery, electricity production from anaerobic digester, compost

AWARD:
Dairy of Distinction

Opposite page:
Back row from left: Claire, David, Denise, Steven, Marjorie, Steven Barstow II; front row from left: Caroline, Shannon, Kelly, and Ann Barstow (and Moose, the dog)

Barstow's Longview Farm's
CHEDDAR-CORN CHOWDER

This rich, savory chowder is on the menu at least monthly, year-round at Barstow's Dairy Store and Bakery quite simply because, as Shannon Barstow says, smiling: "If we don't serve it, we get yelled at."

4 thick slices bacon, chopped

2 Tbsp. butter

3 cups chopped onion

¼ cup all-purpose flour

1 tsp. table salt

½ tsp. black pepper

¼ tsp. ground turmeric

6 cups chicken stock

3 cups diced unpeeled white potato

4 cups fresh corn kernels or 1 (16-oz.) bag frozen corn kernels, unthawed

2 cups (8 oz.) shredded sharp Cheddar, plus more for garnish

1 cup half-and-half

Sliced green onions, optional

COOK bacon in a Dutch oven set over medium-high heat, stirring often, 6 minutes or until crisp; remove bacon with a slotted spoon, and drain on paper towels, reserving drippings in Dutch oven.

MELT butter in hot drippings. Add onion; cook 8 minutes or until tender, stirring occasionally.

STIR in flour, salt, pepper, and turmeric. Cook, stirring constantly, 3 minutes. Stir in chicken stock and potato. Bring to a boil; cover, reduce heat, and simmer 18 minutes or until potato is tender.

STIR in corn, Cheddar, and half-and-half. Bring to a simmer; cook 5 minutes or just until cheese melts. (Do not boil.)

SEASON with salt and pepper. Ladle soup into bowls. Top with bacon, Cheddar, and green onions, if using.

MAKES 8 servings

 KITCHEN WISDOM To cut kernels from fresh ears of corn with the least mess, cut the end of the cob off as evenly as you can. Place the bottom of the cob in the center of a clean kitchen towel, and carefully cut down each side with a sharp knife, rotating the cob, so that the kernels fall onto the towel.

LENTIL-VEGGIE SOUP
WITH CHEDDAR CROUTONS

2   (15-oz.) cans lentils, drained

1   (14 -oz.) can vegetable broth (1¾ cups)

1½ cups diced mixed cooked vegetables

½   tsp. dried oregano, crumbled

½   tsp. dried thyme leaves, crumbled

8   thin slices baguette

½   cup (2 oz.) shredded sharp Cheddar
    or extra sharp Cheddar

POUR lentils into a large saucepan, and partially mash with a potato masher or wooden spoon to break up some of lentils, which will thicken the soup.

ADD broth, vegetables, oregano, and thyme, and bring to a simmer over medium-high heat. Cook, stirring often, 5 minutes.

MEANWHILE, preheat broiler. Arrange bread slices on a baking sheet, and top each with 1 Tbsp. cheese. Place under broiler until cheese is browned in spots.

SEASON soup with salt and pepper. Serve soup with croutons floated on top.

MAKES 4 servings

This hearty soup is great for using up leftover cooked vegetables and can be on the table in less than 10 minutes. If you don't have any pre-cooked vegetables, chop up zucchini, broccoli, bell peppers, and sweet potatoes, and roast them with a little olive oil in the oven at 450° for 15 minutes, stirring once.

BUTTERNUT SQUASH AND SAGE BISQUE

A beautiful shade of orange flecked with fresh sage and spiked with sunny orange juice and Greek-style yogurt, this soup tastes and looks delicious. And it's good for you as well!

1　medium (2-lb.) butternut squash

3　cups reduced-sodium chicken or vegetable broth

1　Tbsp. chopped fresh sage

¼　cup milk

¼　cup plain Greek-style yogurt

2　Tbsp. orange juice

Thinly sliced fresh sage leaves for garnish, optional

PREHEAT oven to 400°. Place uncut squash on a baking sheet, and bake 1 hour or until squash gives all over to soft pressure of your fingertips. Cool; slice in half lengthwise. Scoop out and discard seeds (or save for later toasting, per tip below).

SCOOP out cooked pulp, about 2½ cups, and puree in a blender or food processor until completely smooth. Scrape into a medium soup pot set over medium-high heat.

WHISK broth and sage into squash puree, and bring to a boil. Reduce heat and simmer 5 minutes, stirring occasionally. Stir in milk, yogurt, and orange juice, and simmer 5 minutes. Season with salt and pepper; serve topped with thinly sliced fresh sage leaves, if using.

MAKES 4 servings

TIP>> If you want to toast your squash seeds, clean them well, and spread them on a baking sheet to dry overnight. For about ½ cup seeds, use 2 tsp. olive oil and 2 tsp. soy sauce. Spread them out again on the baking sheet, and roast at 350° for 7 to 8 minutes, until dark golden and toasty. If you hear them start to pop in the oven, they're done!

CHEESY TACO SOUP

1   lb. lean ground turkey

Pinch of table salt

2   Tbsp. butter

2   Tbsp. all-purpose flour

2½ cups milk, divided

1   cup (4 oz.) shredded Monterey Jack

1½ tsp. onion powder

1½ tsp. chili powder

1   tsp. ground cumin

1   tsp. garlic powder

1   tsp. dried oregano

1   (15-oz.) can black beans, drained and rinsed

1   (10-oz.) can diced tomatoes and green chiles, undrained

Crushed tortilla chips and sour cream or plain Greek-style yogurt to serve

Chopped fresh cilantro, optional

COOK ground turkey with a pinch of salt in a large soup pot set over medium-high heat, stirring to break up beef until browned and thoroughly cooked, about 5 to 7 minutes. Pour off any excess drippings and set pot with turkey in it aside.

MELT butter in a small saucepan set over medium heat. Whisk in flour, and cook 1 minute. Slowly whisk in 1 cup milk. Using a wooden spoon, stir mixture until thickened, about 3 to 4 minutes. Remove from heat, and stir in cheese until smooth; set aside.

WHISK together onion powder, chili powder, cumin, garlic powder, and oregano in a small bowl.

RETURN pot with turkey to medium heat and stir in spice mix; cook about 1 minute until fragrant. Stir in black beans, diced tomatoes and green chiles, and remaining 1½ cups milk. Add cheese sauce, and stir well to combine. Bring just to a simmer; reduce heat and simmer 10 minutes, stirring occasionally.

SERVE topped with crushed tortilla chips and sour cream or plain Greek-style yogurt and cilantro, if using.

MAKES 4 to 6 servings

A stick-to-your-ribs dish with hearty flavor and texture, this taco soup hits the spot on a cold, wet day.

TIP>> If you prefer, you can substitute 1 (1.25-oz.) package taco seasoning mix for the spices.

Worthen Dairy Farm

MERCER, MAINE

FARM FAMILY:
Jonas and Mellori
Worthen

YEARS OWNED:
165 years
[since 1850]

FARMSTEAD:
About 500
acres, including 445
acres of woods

HERD:
40 Holsteins

**OTHER FARM
BUSINESS:**
Egg sales

WORTHEN DAIRY FARM IS AS OLD-SCHOOL AS the coal-fired cast-iron stove over which Mellori Worthen cooks many of the family's meals. Or the fact that Jonas Worthen pretty much handles everything by himself on the small 40-cow dairy, including twice daily milkings into buckets.

That means that it's been decades since Jonas has left the farm for longer than 12 hours, the time between milkings. His teenage son and wife, who is a musician and music teacher, take daytrips and occasionally overnights around her summer schedule of wedding gigs, and Jonas is sometimes able to join them for part of the day. But the Worthens have never taken a family vacation. Despite that, Jonas says, "I always wanted to stay on the farm. I like farming because you're more free than with a regular job." Looking over at their son, Mellori says cheerfully, "One day when he takes over, we'll go on a monthlong honeymoon."

Andrew, 14, has been a part of the farm's rhythms since he was born. "His first memories are bumping along in the tractor," says Mellori. Andrew helps with feeding and naming the cows. "They head-butt me," he says with a chuckle. He plans to attend a local high school with an agriculture program.

Although Jonas knows some people might view farming as repetitive, he appreciates its variety. "Every season has a different job," he says. "Spring is building and machinery repairs, top-dressing fields with manure, starting seeds for the garden, checking the fencing," he says. Late spring means the lilacs bloom. In early June, the cows go out on pasture. "The first day out they're jumping," Andrew pipes up. "They're so excited to go out!"

Summer and fall mean haying, chopping grass, and a riot of peas, tomatoes, corn, beans, potatoes, and onions to be tended, harvested, and preserved throughout. "I start as soon as the rhubarb's up," Mellori says. She cans everything from green tomato mincemeat and peach-rhubarb pie filling to tomato salsa, and she cooks with that home-grown goodness all through the winter, including dessert every day. "They'd eat it three times a day if they could," she says with a fond smile, looking over at her husband and son.

Andrew, Jonas, and
Mellori Worthen

Andrew Worthen's
CHICKEN AND VEGETABLE GARDEN CHILI

1   Tbsp. chili powder

1½ tsp. ground cumin

1   tsp. table salt

1   tsp. dried oregano

1   tsp. ground coriander

4   skinned and boned chicken breasts (about 2 lb.), cut into ½-inch cubes

2   Tbsp. canola oil

2   (16-oz.) jars mild or medium salsa

1   lb. fresh green beans, trimmed and cut into 1-inch pieces

1   (15.8-oz.) can Great Northern beans, drained and rinsed

1   (14.5-oz.) can diced tomatoes with garlic and onion, undrained

2   cups fresh (3 ears) or frozen corn kernels

1   cup cooked brown rice

½   cup chopped fresh cilantro

Shredded extra sharp Cheddar, sour cream or plain Greek-style yogurt, tortilla chips, and chopped fresh cilantro to serve, optional

COMBINE chili powder, cumin, salt, dried oregano, and coriander in a shallow dish. Dredge chicken in spice mixture until coated on all sides.

HEAT oil in a large Dutch oven over medium-high heat. Brown chicken in hot oil 5 minutes, stirring often.

ADD salsa, green beans, Great Northern beans, diced tomatoes, corn, and brown rice, stirring to loosen browned bits from bottom of Dutch oven. Bring to a boil; reduce heat, and simmer, partially covered, 40 minutes, stirring occasionally. (Alternatively, you can also transfer browned chicken to a slow cooker. Add salsa, green beans, Great Northern beans, diced tomatoes, corn, and brown rice, and cook on LOW 5 to 6 hours.)

STIR in ½ cup fresh cilantro, and ladle chili into bowls. Serve with toppings, if using.

MAKES 8 servings

Farmer's son Andrew Worthen is known around his hometown for his chicken and vegetable chili, which he first made when he was seven. It is chock-full of vegetables from the family's garden, fresh in summer and canned the rest of the year.

SAVORY HERB CORN MUFFINS

These colorful corn muffins are loaded with a fresh confetti of vegetables, as well as light Cheddar and Greek-style yogurt. Not your average corn muffins, they add flavor and color to breakfast and perfectly complement a hot cup of soup or bowl of chili.

1⅓ cups all-purpose flour

1 cup finely ground cornmeal

3 Tbsp. sugar

2 Tbsp. baking powder

1½ tsp. dried thyme leaves, crumbled

½ tsp. table salt

½ tsp. dried rosemary, crumbled

1½ cups (6 oz.) shredded Sharp Extra Light Cheddar, plus more for topping

⅔ cup plain Greek-style yogurt

4 Tbsp. melted butter or vegetable oil

2 large eggs

¼ cup milk

1½ tsp. olive oil

½ cup finely diced onion

½ cup finely diced mushrooms

½ cup finely diced red bell pepper

1 cup chopped fresh spinach

PREHEAT oven to 400°. Coat insides and top of a 12-cup muffin pan with cooking spray.

WHISK together flour, cornmeal, sugar, baking powder, thyme, salt, and rosemary in a large bowl. Stir in 1½ cups shredded Cheddar. Whisk together yogurt, melted butter or vegetable oil, eggs, and milk in another large bowl.

HEAT olive oil in a medium skillet set over medium-high heat. Add onion, mushrooms, and bell pepper, and cook, stirring often, until tender, about 5 minutes. Add spinach and cook until spinach wilts, 1 to 2 minutes longer.

STIR cooked vegetables into yogurt mixture; stir yogurt-vegetable mixture into dry ingredients just until no dry pockets remain. Fill each muffin cup about two-thirds full. Top with remaining shredded Cheddar.

BAKE 15 to 20 minutes or until golden brown on top and a wooden pick inserted in center comes out clean.

MAKES 12 muffins

 TIP>> To save a little more time, use 1 (14- to 17-oz.) box of corn muffin mix in place of the flour, cornmeal, sugar, baking powder, and salt. You can also skip the 4 Tbsp. melted butter or vegetable oil added with the wet ingredients, since the packaged mixes already contain the shortening.

MAY LEACH'S
FOUR BEAN–FOUR PEPPER CHILI

For nearly 30 years, May Leach has played a vital role in quality assurance and new product development at Cabot. She is also a passionate cook who makes this chili regularly for her young grandson, Zac, who loves his food really hot. Zac is also vegetarian, but substitute a pound of ground beef for a can of beans, if you like.

1   Tbsp. coconut oil or vegetable oil

1   large onion, diced

Pinch of table salt

1   jalapeño pepper, seeded, membranes removed, and minced

1   habanero pepper, seeded, membranes removed, and minced

1   Anaheim pepper (or other mild pepper of your choice), seeded and minced

2   bell peppers, color of choice, seeded and diced

4   to 6 garlic cloves, minced

2   to 3 Tbsp. chili powder

1   to 2 Tbsp. ancho chili powder

1   tsp. ground cumin

1   (28-oz.) can diced tomatoes, undrained

1   (28-oz.) can petite diced tomatoes, undrained

4   (15.5-oz.) cans of beans (your choice of black, red, white, or pinto), undrained

¼   cup unsweetened cocoa

Sour cream or plain Greek-style yogurt, diced sweet onion, lime wedges, shredded Hot Habanero Cheddar or sharp Cheddar for topping, optional

HEAT oil in a large stock pot set over medium heat. Add onion with a pinch of salt, and cook until lightly caramelized, about 9 minutes. (If using beef, add here and cook until browned, about 7 to 9 minutes, stirring occasionally to break up meat.) Add peppers and cook until softened, about 5 minutes, seasoning with another small pinch of salt. Add garlic and cook until fragrant, about 1 minute.

STIR in chili powders and cumin, and cook 2 to 3 minutes or until vegetables are well coated with spices. Add canned tomatoes and beans. Stir in unsweetened cocoa, and increase heat to medium-high to bring the chili to a simmer.

REDUCE heat to maintain a simmer, and cook, with cover slightly ajar, 1 to 2 hours, stirring occasionally to prevent sticking. Check seasoning and heat levels; add salt and additional chili powder to taste. Serve in bowls with toppings, if using.

MAKES 8 to 10 servings

CHEDDAR SODA BREAD

2½ cups all-purpose flour

2   tsp. baking powder

1   tsp. baking soda

½   tsp. table salt

4   Tbsp. cold butter, cut into pieces

2   cups (8 oz.) shredded sharp Cheddar
     or extra sharp Cheddar

1   cup buttermilk

1   large egg

PREHEAT oven to 375°. Coat a baking sheet with cooking spray.

WHISK together flour, baking powder, baking soda, and salt in a large bowl. Add butter and work in with fingertips until mixture looks crumbly. Add cheese; toss to combine.

WHISK together buttermilk and egg in a small bowl. Add to flour mixture, and stir until well combined. Turn dough out onto a floured surface. Knead several times, and then shape into a smooth ball. Transfer to prepared baking sheet.

BAKE 35 to 40 minutes or until golden and a long wooden pick inserted in center comes out clean. Serve warm or at room temperature, cut into wedges.

MAKES 1 loaf for about 12 servings

A warm loaf of goodness, this bread pulls together in a jiffy and pairs deliciously with any soup, stew, or chili. Present the whole loaf on a cutting board with soft butter, and wait for the applause.

 **KITCHEN WISDOM** If you don't have buttermilk around, you can substitute ⅓ cup milk whisked with ⅔ cup plain Greek-style yogurt. If you don't have yogurt, you can stir 1 Tbsp. white vinegar or fresh lemon juice into a scant cup of milk and let it sit 5 minutes to curdle slightly.

Liberty Hill Farm's **TURKEY POT PIE**

Biscuits

6 cups all-purpose flour

¾ cup sugar

¼ cup baking powder

1½ tsp. table salt

1 cup cold butter, cut into pieces

1 cup (4 oz.) shredded sharp Cheddar

2 cups very cold 1% low-fat milk

Filling

4 cups diced cooked turkey or chicken

3 cups turkey or chicken gravy (thin with broth or water, if needed)

1 cup cooked vegetables (such as peas and diced carrots, green beans, onions, celery, or fennel)

PREPARE BISCUITS: Preheat oven to 425°. Whisk together flour, sugar, baking powder, and salt in a large bowl. Work butter into dry ingredients with a pastry blender or fork until mixture is crumbly with some small pea-size bits of butter. Stir in Cheddar. Gradually stir in milk.

TURN dough out onto a well-floured surface, and knead gently just until dough comes together. (Do not overwork.) Roll out to 1-inch thickness. Cut out biscuits with a 2- to 3-inch round cutter or small glass. Reroll extra dough, and cut to use it all up.

PREPARE FILLING: Stir together turkey or chicken, gravy, and vegetables in a large saucepan set over medium heat until hot. Transfer to a 13- x 9-inch baking dish, making sure turkey is covered with gravy. Arrange biscuits about ½ inch apart in rows across top of hot filling. Place any extra biscuits on a baking sheet.

BAKE pot pie and biscuits about 15 minutes or until biscuits are golden. Serve immediately.

MAKES 8 servings

In Maine, where Beth Kennett grew up, pot pie is topped with a pastry crust. In Vermont, as she soon learned, pot pies have biscuits on top. Beth is famous for her Cheddar biscuits, and here, crowning bubbling turkey and vegetables in savory gravy, they complete the kind of homey, comforting meal that guests enjoy at Liberty Hill Farm (*see profile on page 74*).

EGGPLANT AND CHICKPEA STEW WITH CHEDDAR DUMPLINGS

This satisfying, different vegetarian main dish features flavorful dumplings that balance the earthiness of the stew.

Stew

3 Tbsp. olive oil

2 large eggplants (2½ to 3 lb. total), peeled and cut into ¾-inch cubes

1 large onion, coarsely chopped

3 medium cloves garlic, thinly sliced

2 (15.5-oz.) cans chickpeas (garbanzo beans), drained

1½ cups crushed tomatoes

1 tsp. table salt

½ tsp. ground black pepper

1 cup frozen corn

1 Tbsp. mild chili powder

1 tsp. ground cumin

Dumplings

¾ cup (3 oz.) shredded Sharp Light, sharp, or extra sharp Cheddar

¾ cup all-purpose flour

¼ cup yellow cornmeal

1 tsp. baking powder

¼ tsp. table salt

¼ cup milk

1 large egg

PREPARE STEW: Heat oil in a large ovenproof pot set over medium heat. Add eggplant, onion, and garlic, and cook, stirring often, until eggplant and onion are lightly golden, about 15 minutes. Toward end of cooking time, place rack in lower third of oven and preheat oven to 350°.

STIR 2 cups water, chickpeas, crushed tomatoes, 1 tsp. salt, and pepper into eggplant mixture, and increase heat to medium-high to bring mixture to a simmer. Cover pot with lid or aluminum foil, and bake 45 to 55 minutes or until eggplant is completely tender. (Stew can be made a day or two ahead up to this point; let cool and refrigerate, and then reheat to simmer, and proceed with recipe.)

PREPARE DUMPLINGS: While stew cooks, toss together Cheddar, flour, cornmeal, baking powder, and ¼ tsp. salt in a medium bowl. Whisk together milk and egg in another small bowl. When stew is ready, stir milk-egg mixture into dry ingredients just until combined.

UNCOVER stew; stir corn, chili powder, and cumin into stew. Add more chili powder and cumin to taste. Add salt and pepper to taste. Drop dumpling mixture in 8 mounds on top of stew. Cover pot and bake about 15 minutes longer or until dumplings are puffed and feel "set" when lightly pressed.

MAKES 8 servings

BEEF STROGANOFF
WITH GREEK-STYLE YOGURT

1	lb. top sirloin steak, cut into 1- x 2-inch strips	2	Tbsp. all-purpose flour
1	Tbsp. olive or vegetable oil	1½	cups reduced-sodium beef broth
3	Tbsp. butter, divided	12	oz. wide whole wheat or regular egg noodles
¼	cup minced shallots or onions	⅔	cup plain Greek-style yogurt
8	oz. baby portobello (cremini) mushrooms, stems trimmed, caps wiped clean and sliced	1	Tbsp. chopped fresh dill
			Sweet smoked paprika or sweet paprika

SEASON steak well with salt and pepper. Heat oil in a large heavy skillet set over high heat until hot and shimmering. Add only as much of the steak as will fit in a single layer with space between pieces, and cook until browned on both sides, about 1 minute per side. Transfer to a plate, and repeat as necessary until all beef is browned; set aside.

ADD 2 Tbsp. butter to skillet, reduce heat to medium, add shallots or onion, and cook until softened, about 2 minutes. Add mushrooms and cook, stirring occasionally, 5 to 7 minutes or until mushrooms have given up their liquid and are tender and golden. Add flour, stirring until blended, about 1 minute longer.

STIR in beef broth, and bring to a simmer, scraping up browned bits from bottom of skillet. Cook 3 to 4 minutes or until thickened, and remove skillet from heat.

PREPARE noodles in a large pot of boiling water according to package directions. Drain and toss with remaining 1 Tbsp. butter. Cover to keep warm.

RETURN skillet with mushrooms and sauce to medium heat, and stir in reserved browned beef and any juices. Cook 5 minutes or until heated through. Take skillet off heat, and stir in yogurt and dill until well blended. Season with salt and pepper. Serve over noodles, sprinkled with paprika.

MAKES 4 servings

Stroganoff is a classic dish featuring seared beef and earthy mushrooms in a flavorful, velvety sauce served over hot noodles. Our take on this favorite retains the familiar robust flavors but has been updated with cremini mushrooms, Greek-style yogurt, and sweet smoked paprika.

MEATBALLS MARINARA WITH CHEDDAR-SPINACH POLENTA

Nothing says Italian-style comfort like a big bowl of steaming meatballs and sauce served over creamy, cheesy polenta with spinach.

Meatballs

⅓ cup 2% reduced-fat milk

¼ cup "instant" (quick-cooking) polenta

1 tsp. dried oregano

1 tsp. dried thyme leaves

1 tsp. minced garlic

½ tsp. table salt

¼ tsp. ground black pepper

1 large egg

1 lb. ground round (85% lean)

1 tsp. olive oil

2 cups marinara sauce

Polenta

¾ tsp. table salt

1 cup "instant" (quick-cooking) polenta

4 cups lightly packed fresh baby spinach or arugula leaves, coarsely chopped

1 cup (4 oz.) shredded mild, Sharp Light, or sharp Cheddar, plus extra for garnish

TIP>> If you can't find "instant" polenta, use 1 cup regular polenta for the Cheddar-spinach polenta. Follow the package cooking directions, but use ⅓ cup fine, dry breadcrumbs in the meatballs instead of polenta.

PREPARE MEATBALLS: Stir together milk, ¼ cup polenta, oregano, thyme, garlic, ½ tsp. salt, and pepper in a small bowl; let stand until milk is absorbed, about 2 minutes.

WHISK egg until frothy in a large bowl. Stir in ground beef and polenta mixture, and mix together well. Divide mixture into 4 equal portions. Shape each portion into 6 (1¼-inch) meatballs, for a total of 24.

HEAT oil in a large skillet set over medium-high heat. Add meatballs, in batches, if necessary, and cook, turning, until browned all over, about 4 to 6 minutes. Reduce heat to low, and add marinara sauce, turning meatballs to coat. Cover skillet with lid or aluminum foil, and let meatballs simmer gently until cooked through to center, about 10 minutes.

PREPARE POLENTA: Bring 4 cups water and ¾ tsp. salt to a boil in a large sauce-pan. Reduce heat to medium-low. Gradually pour in 1 cup polenta, stirring constantly; stir in spinach or arugula. Continue stirring until polenta has absorbed all of the water and is simmering and thickened, about 3 minutes. Stir in 1 cup Cheddar.

SPOON polenta onto a platter or into shallow bowls; top with meatballs and sauce. Garnish with remaining cheese, if using.

MAKES 4 to 6 servings

CORN-CHEDDAR RISOTTO WITH SHRIMP

4 cups fat-free chicken broth

½ tsp. dried thyme leaves or 3 sprigs fresh thyme

1½ lb. unpeeled raw shrimp

1 Tbsp. butter

¾ cup chopped onion

1¼ cups Arborio rice

2 cups fresh or frozen corn kernels

1 cup (4 oz.) shredded Sharp Light or Sharp Extra Light Cheddar

3 Tbsp. chopped fresh parsley

Risotto is warm, creamy, and comforting, but it is also probably the most elegant dish that is ever served in a bowl, especially when it stars shrimp.

BRING broth and thyme to a simmer in a large saucepan. Add shrimp, return to a simmer, and cook until shrimp are just firm, about 2 minutes. With a slotted spoon, transfer shrimp to a bowl, setting broth aside, covered to keep warm. (Remove whole sprigs of thyme if you used them.) Fill bowl with cold water to cool shrimp, and then drain, peel, and set aside.

MELT butter in a large pot set over medium-low heat. Add onion and cook, stirring often, until softened, about 3 minutes. Add rice and stir 2 minutes.

ADD ½ cup of reserved warm broth, adjusting heat to maintain a gentle simmer and stirring often. When broth is absorbed, add another ½ cup, repeating until all broth is used (cooking time will be about 20 minutes total). Rice should still be slightly firm but not crunchy in center; add hot water a half cup at a time if rice needs further cooking.

STIR in corn and reserved shrimp; stir until heated through, about 2 minutes. Stir in Cheddar and parsley. Season with salt and pepper.

MAKES 6 servings

 TIP>> Cooking the unpeeled shrimp in the chicken broth adds great seafood flavor to the dish. For a quicker version, you can purchase peeled cooked shrimp and make the risotto with plain chicken broth heated with the thyme.

Spicy Cheddar Burgers, page 143

Midday Break

SANDWICHES, BURGERS, WRAPS, AND ROLLUPS

"Ever since I can remember, my grandparents were adamant that we have lunch with them every day."

—Cricket Jacquier, Laurel Brook Farm
East Canaan, Connecticut

grilled cheese, please!

Every Cabot farm family has favorite grilled cheese combinations, and at Tiashoke Farms, Jessica Ziehm's go-to pairing is extra sharp Cheddar with apple butter and thin slices of crisp, local apples, "something my mother always made for me as a kid," she recalls fondly. Her husband,

SANDWICH	BREAD	SPREAD
1 HEAVEN IN VERMONT	whole wheat	
2 TIASHOKE FARM GIRL'S FAVE	oatmeal	apple butter
3 STUART'S SPICY SPECIAL	sourdough	
4 UNIVERSITY OF VERMONT'S *CREAM* CHEESE SANDWICH	hearty country	basil pesto
5 ST. PADDY'S SPECIAL	oatmeal or multigrain	
6 SMOKY CHIPOTLE AND CHORIZO	hearty semolina	Chipotle Aïoli (see recipe, page 143)
7 NECTARINE AND BACON JAM	whole grain	Bacon Jam (see recipe, page 125)

You can use regular pesto or Cheddar-Walnut Pesto (see recipe, page 125).

Use baby spinach for a tender, healthy extra!

Stuart, on the other hand, is a fan of all that is spicy and pickled. His favorite combination mixes shredded Hot Habanero Cheddar with a little mayonnaise and pickled jalapeño juice, topped with some pickled jalapeños. You might want a tall glass of something cold to wash that down.

CHEESE	OTHER INGREDIENTS
Seriously Sharp	applewood smoked bacon maple syrup
Extra Sharp	sliced apple, such as Empire
¼ cup Hot Habanero Cheddar mixed with 2 tsp. mayonnaise and 1 tsp. pickled jalapeño juice	pickled jalapeño slices
Seriously Sharp	baby spinach
Sharp	coleslaw mix stirred with Thousand Island or honey-mustard dressing corned beef
Chipotle Cheddar	cooked, crumbled chorizo sausage
Vintage Choice Extra Sharp	sliced nectarines

GREAT GRILLED CHEESE

WITH ITS CRISPY, BUTTERY EXTERIOR and melted cheese filling, grilled cheese makes a perfect snack, lunch, or light supper with a salad or soup. The sky's the limit when it comes to fillings; the only requirements are two slices of bread and cheese. There are, however, a few key tips for making the best grilled cheese.

Rachel Freund, the youngest in the Freund's Farm family (see page 126), recently graduated from the University of Vermont, where she volunteered with FeelGood, a student-run grilled cheese stand from which 100 percent of the proceeds go to The Hunger Project, an international nonprofit working to end hunger and poverty by pioneering sustainable, grassroots, women-centered strategies. Rachel also worked with the university's student-run dairy herd, named CREAM—Cooperative for Real Education in Agricultural Management—one of a number of educational dairy herds that are Cabot members. The FeelGood stand has a regular menu, but it also runs weekly themed specials like a late-spring Earth Day special featuring sliced roasted winter squash, caramelized onions, Cheddar, and a drizzle of maple syrup, or, in honor of Dr. Seuss's birthday, pesto-scrambled green eggs with Cheddar.

Rachel's TIPS >>

Rachel Freund shared some of her expert grilled cheese tips:

THINK THIN. Don't use bread slices that are too thick or your cheese won't melt at the same rate as the sandwich browns, and the bread might also overwhelm your filling. Standard sliced bread works fine; if you're slicing your own, keep it under ½ inch thick.

For an extra-buttery crisp exterior, you can spread the exterior of each piece of bread with a thin, even coating of softened butter.

For optimal melted cheese, use thin slices, or do as the FeelGood student volunteers do—use about ¼ cup cheese crumbles or shreds for each sandwich.

PRESS IT! After you have added remaining fillings, place second slice of bread on top, and press down firmly to settle your sandwich. Whatever tool you use to "grill" your sandwich, you will get the best results from applying pressure while it cooks. A panini press or two-sided contact indoor electric grill, like the FeelGood volunteers use, will do that work for you.

BE PATIENT. Cook your sandwich slowly over medium-low heat until golden on underside, reducing heat if needed, 2 to 4 minutes. Turn and cook until golden on second side and cheese is melted, another 2 to 4 minutes.

ENJOY! Cut sandwiches in half, and serve immediately, or for a grilled cheese on the go, wrap the bottom with aluminum foil to make a handy, drip-preventing portable pocket.

BACON JAM

1   lb. sliced bacon

4   leeks, tops removed, cut in half,
    thinly sliced, and cleaned, or about
    2 cups coarsely chopped sweet onion

2   tsp. chopped garlic

½   cup firmly packed dark brown sugar

½   cup apple cider vinegar

½   cup bourbon or apple cider

2   Tbsp. honey

1   tsp. Dijon mustard

COOK bacon in a large skillet over medium-high heat until crisp; remove bacon, and drain on paper towels, reserving 1 Tbsp. drippings in skillet. Coarsely chop bacon and set aside.

ADD leeks or onion and garlic to skillet over medium heat; cook, stirring occasionally, until softened, about 4 to 5 minutes.

ADD brown sugar, vinegar, bourbon or cider, honey, and mustard to skillet. Bring mixture to a boil; then reduce heat, and simmer until thickened, stirring occasionally, about 5 minutes. Stir in reserved bacon. Scrape bacon-leek mixture into the bowl of a food processor, and pulse until very finely chopped and fairly smooth. Store in refrigerator up to 2 weeks.

MAKES 1 cup

Smoky with a sweet-tart balance, this "jam" elevates simple grilled cheese and adds layers of flavor to the standard BLT&C (with Cheddar, of course).

CHEDDAR-WALNUT PESTO

2   cups loosely packed washed and dried
    fresh basil leaves

½   cup (2 oz.) shredded sharp Cheddar

¼   cup chopped walnuts

1   Tbsp. fresh lemon juice

1   large clove garlic, roughly chopped

1   tsp. table salt

½   tsp. freshly ground black pepper

6   Tbsp. extra virgin olive oil

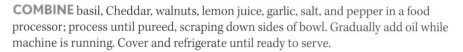

COMBINE basil, Cheddar, walnuts, lemon juice, garlic, salt, and pepper in a food processor; process until pureed, scraping down sides of bowl. Gradually add oil while machine is running. Cover and refrigerate until ready to serve.

MAKES about ¾ cup

Our Cheddar twist on basil pesto has enough flavor to be a sandwich filling all by itself, but try it on bread with spinach or arugula and roasted sliced turkey.

Freund's Farm

EAST CANAAN, CONNECTICUT

From left: Cole Van Seters,
Theresa Freund, Matt Freund,
Isaac Freund, Rachel Freund,
Ben Freund, and Amanda Freund

FARMERS ARE ADEPT AT MAKING DO WITH WHAT'S ON HAND, but Freund's Farm just might win the prize for the most creative example with their CowPots: patented, biodegradable, seed-starter pots made from composted, odorless manure generated by the farm's 280-head dairy herd. Manure management is one of the biggest challenges faced by dairy farmers, but the Freund family uses a methane digester to produce valuable fertilizer, CowPot materials, and renewable power. "Doing the best we can for the environment has always been a high priority for our farm," explains Matt Freund, who, with his brother Ben, took over from their mother, Esther, and father, Eugene.

The Freunds minimize the use of chemicals on their fields. They've installed more than 500 solar panels to generate additional renewable energy and even recycle brewers' grain as part of their animal feed. The flowerpot idea was a decade in the making, starting with crude compost and glue pots baked in a toaster oven; it evolved into a product that has been featured on national television from the *Today* show to CNN. CowPots are now sold at retail stores around the country and shipped globally, generating a significant income for the farm.

Matt and his wife, Theresa, have worked hard to build a diversified business. In addition to the CowPots and the dairy, the farm has a busy market, bakery, and catering operation that make delicious use of what Theresa and her crew grow on 15 acres and in extensive greenhouses. The market bursts with homegrown goodness from cranberry-apple butter to frozen quiches, along with baskets of sweet corn, tomatoes, and squashes, plus a rainbow of fresh-cut flowers. The family dinner table is similarly weighed down with fresh-baked bread, homemade applesauce, corn casserole, caramelized Brussels sprouts, and maybe a pork roast served with Theresa's signature ginger-spiked plum gumbo chutney.

They feel lucky their children seem inclined to stay involved. The younger Freunds all left for studies and work, but like their parents and uncle, they were pulled back by the farm. "It's the place I like being most," says Isaac. Every so often, Matt says, the family takes a walk after dinner. "We head up to the pond and see the cows on pasture. The sun is setting, and we walk by my brother's house. It's a nice time to reflect. It definitely feels good to have your kids proud of what you do—and that the town appreciates us being here, those things give me a sense of accomplishment."

FARM FAMILY:
Brothers Ben and Matt Freund with Matt's wife, Theresa, and their kids, Amanda, Rachel and Isaac

YEARS OWNED:
62 years [since 1953]

FARMSTEAD:
455 acres, about half wooded

HERD:
280 Holsteins and 2 Jerseys

OTHER FARM BUSINESS:
CowPots, farmstand, bakery and catering

AWARDS:
Connecticut Conservation Award 1988, Green Pastures Connecticut Outstanding Dairy Farm of the Year 1983 and 2003, Connecticut Quality Improvement Award Innovation Prize 2010, CowPots received Direct Gardening Association's Green Thumbs Award 2007

THE VER-MONTE CRISTO

Based loosely on the French *croque monsieur*, the Vermont version of this fried ham-and-cheese sandwich is rich and delicious. For a fully Green Mountain State experience, eat it drizzled with pure maple syrup.

1	large egg
½	cup half-and-half
1	Tbsp. pure vanilla extract
4	slices favorite local bread, thinly sliced
2	Tbsp. butter, divided
½	Granny Smith apple, sliced

1	whole shallot or very small onion, thinly sliced
1	tsp. apple cider vinegar
1	cup (4 oz.) shredded sharp Cheddar
2	cooked sausage patties or thick slices ham

WHISK together egg, half-and-half, and vanilla in a shallow bowl. Add bread slices, turning to coat with mixture, and set aside to soak.

MELT 1 Tbsp. butter in a small skillet set over medium-high heat; add apple slices and shallot or onion, and cook until tender, stirring occasionally, about 7 to 9 minutes. Add vinegar and cook 1 minute longer. Set aside.

MELT remaining 1 Tbsp. butter in a large skillet set over medium heat. Remove bread slices from egg mixture (discard remaining egg mixture), and cook 2 minutes on one side.

TAKE skillet off heat, and flip 2 of the bread slices uncooked sides down. Sprinkle each with ¼ cup Cheddar; then add sausage patty or ham slice topped with half of the apple mixture. Top each with ¼ cup Cheddar and a second slice of bread, cooked side down.

PLACE skillet back over medium heat, and cook about 2 minutes or until golden on underside. Turn sandwiches over, and cook 2 minutes longer or until golden on second side and cheese is melted. Cut in half, and serve warm.

MAKES 2 sandwiches

TRY SOMETHING *different*

For a simpler and lighter version we call Cheddar Cheese Dreams, make sandwiches first with your choice of bread spread lightly with mustard and topped with thinly sliced Cheddar of your choice and smoked turkey breast. Press sandwiches together firmly. Whisk together 2 eggs with ⅓ cup milk (enough for 4 sandwiches), and briefly soak each side of sandwich in the mixture before cooking in skillet per step 5 above.

Rachel Freund and
Cole Van Seters

GRIDDLED RACHEL SANDWICHES

2   Tbsp. ketchup
2   Tbsp. light mayonnaise
2   tsp. dill pickle relish
Pinch of celery seed, optional
½   cup sauerkraut, excess moisture squeezed out

2   Tbsp. butter, softened
4   slices rye bread
4   oz. thinly sliced cooked turkey
½   cup (2 oz.) shredded Alpine Blend, extra sharp Cheddar, or Monterey Jack

A great mixture of tangy, salty, and savory comes together in this substantial hot griddled sandwich, which plays off the classic deli-style Reuben.

WHISK together ketchup, mayonnaise, relish, and celery seed, if using, in a small bowl.

PLACE sauerkraut in a small, microwave-safe dish, and microwave at HIGH 1 to 2 minutes or until steaming hot; set aside.

SPREAD butter over one side of each bread slice. Turn slices over, and spread each with ketchup-mayonnaise mixture.

TOP 2 bread slices with turkey, sauerkraut, and cheese. Top with remaining bread slices, buttered sides up.

PLACE a large skillet over medium-low heat; add sandwiches and cook until golden on undersides, about 4 minutes. Turn over and cook until sandwiches are golden on second side and cheese is melted, about 2 minutes longer.

MAKES 2 sandwiches

MARGARITA MARTINEZ'S GRILLED CHEESE WITH RED ONION, APPLE, AND APRICOT JAM

Special Cabot spokesperson Margarita Martinez, who is also a New Englander, likes to make this grilled cheese with apples, Dijon mustard, apricot jam, and two kinds of Cheddar.

3   Tbsp. olive oil, divided
1   small red onion, very thinly sliced into half-moons
1   small apple, very thinly sliced
4   slices hearty whole grain bread
2   Tbsp. Dijon mustard

2   Tbsp. apricot jam
2   slices Sharp Light Cheddar
2   slices Vintage Choice Cheddar
Additional raw apple slices, optional
Mixed salad greens to serve

HEAT 1 Tbsp. olive oil in a large skillet set over medium-high heat. Add a single layer of onion slices to skillet, and cook until slightly softened and golden; remove to a plate.

ADD apple slices to skillet with a little more olive oil as needed, and cook until softened and golden; remove to another plate.

REDUCE heat to low. Coat skillet again with 1 Tbsp. olive oil. Add bread slices, and toast lightly on one side for 2 minutes.

SPREAD each untoasted side lightly with mustard and jam. Top 2 of the slices with light Cheddar slices. Cover skillet with lid or aluminum foil just until Cheddar is melted, 2 to 3 minutes.

ADD Vintage Choice Cheddar slices on top of light Cheddar. Top each with half the cooked apple slices, adding a few raw apple slices for crunch, if using. Top each with half the cooked onion slices.

PLACE remaining 2 toasted bread slices on top with mustard-jam sides down, and press firmly to compress sandwiches. Cover skillet and cook 3 to 4 minutes, just until Vintage Choice Cheddar melts. Serve sandwiches on a bed of mixed salad greens.

MAKES 2 sandwiches

Tiashoke Farms

CAMBRIDGE, NEW YORK

From left: Jessica holding daughter Phoebe, Stuart, Eric, Frank, Terry, and Brian Ziehm

SITTING AT THE FARMHOUSE KITCHEN TABLE, Jessica Ziehm jokes, "Some people have a wine refrigerator; we have one in the basement just for cheese." Jessica is married to Stuart, the youngest of the three Ziehm sons, who together make up the fourth generation of farmers in the family, the third working the land where Stuart's grandfather moved in 1966 from his original farm in the Albany suburbs. He was looking for more land and water, and, once he found it, Tiashoke (the Native American name means "meeting of the waters") was born. The family's regular gatherings, replete with a happy tumble of cousins, always start with cheese and crackers before moving on to hearty, home-style meals of the farm's own beef or pork roasts, served perhaps with a favorite cheesy hash brown casserole and local sweet corn.

The farm has grown considerably since the childhood days of Stuart and his brothers, Brian and Eric, and now provides a living for four families, including their parents Frank and Terry. Frank pushed his sons to explore life off the family farm, but they all came back. Stuart worked in California and Pennsylvania on operations milking thousands of cows. "As big and bright as all those other opportunities were, no opportunity was bigger and brighter than coming home to work with family and share this lifestyle," he says. Once the brothers were ready, Frank handed over the reins, although he remains very much involved. "Dad really understood the value of an early farm transition," Stuart says. "That can be one of hardest hurdles for American farm families: protecting the older generation and providing for the next generation."

In addition to milking 1,100 and raising almost an equal number of heifers, the Ziehms grow feed crops on more than 1,600 acres and are constantly refining their approach to improve both their systems and the life/work balance for everyone, including their employees—"to grow so we can support everyone and not work harder, but smarter and better," Stuart explains. The family members all love farming's connections to animals and the land, but they also appreciate the business aspects. "We get to work in and around what we create," Stuart says. "These are our ideas. We're entrepreneurs." He acknowledges, "Things have changed. There's more big equipment, and it's more

FARM FAMILY:
Frank and Terry Ziehm with sons Brian, Eric and Stuart

YEARS OWNED:
49 [since 1966]

FARMSTEAD:
More than 1,600 acres

HERD:
2,000 Holsteins

OTHER FARM BUSINESS:
Pumpkin patch

AWARD:
Dairy of Distinction

challenging to include the children in everything we do, but we don't want them to miss the opportunity to catch the fever." The farm's 10-acre pumpkin patch provides a perfect opportunity for the next generation to get involved. Many hands make lighter work in the field followed by the busy fall harvest and farmstand season. And if Stuart and Jessica's eldest is any indication, the farming bug has tagged another generation. With ruddy cheeks, yellow farm boots, and his own pair of work gloves, 4-year-old Franklin guides a full tour of the herd and barns, showing healthy respect for big animals and big gates, enthusiasm for the energetic calves, and detouring only twice to climb into a tractor seat.

BBQ PORK BURGERS
WITH BACON AND MONTEREY JACK

3   slices smoky bacon

½   yellow onion, finely chopped

1   lb. ground pork

3   Tbsp. plus ½ cup thick tomato-based barbecue sauce, divided

1   to 1½ tsp. hot sauce, to taste

½   tsp. table salt

4   slices (about 4 oz.) Monterey Jack

4   soft onion rolls

This super-savory burger brings together the smoky goodness of bacon and ground pork. Top it with barbecue sauce for more deep flavor.

COOK bacon in a small skillet set over medium-high heat until crisp; remove bacon, and drain on paper towels, reserving 2 tsp. drippings in skillet. Finely chop bacon, and set aside in a medium bowl.

ADD onion to skillet, and cook, stirring occasionally, until soft and translucent, about 3 to 5 minutes. Spread on a small plate to cool.

PREHEAT grill to 350° to 400° (medium-high) heat. Add ground pork to bacon in bowl along with 3 Tbsp. barbecue sauce, hot sauce, salt, and cooked onions; mix gently to combine. Shape into 4 (¾-inch-thick) patties.

BRUSH grill with a paper towel dipped in oil to prevent sticking. Brushing with remaining ½ cup barbecue sauce, grill burgers until cooked through to center, 5 to 8 minutes per side.

TOP with cheese, and cover with grill lid or aluminum foil until cheese is melted, about 1 minute. Serve on rolls.

MAKES 4 burgers

TRY SOMETHING *different*

ON THE GRILL

To grill burgers, preheat grill to 350° to 400° (medium-high) heat. Mix and shape burgers. Brush grill with a paper towel dipped in oil to prevent sticking. Grill burgers until cooked through to center, 5 to 8 minutes per side. Top with cheese, and cover with grill lid or aluminum foil until cheese is melted, about 1 minute.

EASY MOIST TURKEY CHEESEBURGERS

1½ lb. ground turkey

½ cup plain Greek-style yogurt, plus more for serving

1 Tbsp. Worcestershire sauce

½ tsp. ground red pepper

1 shallot, finely diced

6 slices (about 6 oz.) Hot Habanero or Jalapeño Light Cheddar or Pepper Jack

6 whole wheat hamburger buns

Baby spinach, sliced avocado, sliced tomato, optional

PLACE a large skillet over medium-high heat.

MIX together turkey, yogurt, Worcestershire sauce, red pepper, and shallot in a medium bowl. Shape mixture into 6 burgers.

REMOVE hot skillet from heat, and coat with cooking spray. Return to heat, and add burgers. Cook 5 minutes.

TURN burgers over, and cook 4 minutes longer or until cooked through to center. Top with cheese slices, cover pan with lid or aluminum foil, and cook until cheese is melted, about 1 minute longer.

SERVE on buns, spread with more yogurt, and top with spinach, avocado, and tomato, if using.

MAKES 6 burgers

Adding Greek-style yogurt to this lightly spiced turkey burger gives it a nice, juicy taste.

KITCHEN WISDOM When shaping patties for any kind of meat burger, you will get a better result the less you handle them. Divide the mixture first into roughly equal portions for the number of burgers you are making. Then gently pat each portion into a disk, indenting the center gently with your thumb to ensure the burgers are not overly thick in the middle, which can cause the edges to overcook before the middle is done.

BLACK BEAN VEGGIE BURGERS

Mashed sweet potato, shredded sharp Cheddar, and whole wheat breadcrumbs pull this delicious bean burger together nicely. Finely diced beets add unexpected texture.

2   Tbsp. olive oil, divided

½   cup finely chopped onion

½   cup finely diced fresh beets, optional, but if omitting beets, increase cooked sweet potato to 1 cup

3   garlic cloves, minced

1   (15-oz.) can black beans, drained and rinsed

½   cup fine, dry whole wheat breadcrumbs, plus more as needed

¼   cup whole wheat flour

2   Tbsp. minced fresh parsley

½   tsp. table salt

½   tsp. ground black pepper

½   tsp. dried thyme leaves

½   tsp. ground coriander

½   cup mashed cooked sweet potato

1¾ cups (7 oz.) shredded Seriously Sharp Cheddar, divided

1½ Tbsp. fresh lemon juice

Whole wheat buns, pita pockets, bell pepper rings, slices tomato, and lettuce leaves, optional

HEAT 1 Tbsp. oil in a medium skillet set over medium-high heat; add onion and diced beets, if using, and sauté until tender but not mushy, stirring occasionally, about 7 minutes. Add garlic and cook until fragrant, 1 to 2 minutes; set aside.

COMBINE beans, ½ cup breadcrumbs, flour, parsley, salt, pepper, thyme, and coriander in a food processor; pulse 5 to 7 times or until combined but mixture still has some texture.

TRANSFER mixture to a large bowl, and add sweet potato, 1 cup Cheddar, lemon juice, and reserved onion mixture. Mix by hand to combine, adding more breadcrumbs as necessary just until you can handle the mixture, and shape it into 6 patties.

HEAT remaining 1 Tbsp. oil in a large skillet over medium-low heat. Cook burgers until browned on both sides and heated through to center, about 8 to 10 minutes; lower heat if necessary.

TOP each burger with about 2 Tbsp. of remaining Cheddar. Serve with buns or pita pockets, bell pepper rings, tomatoes, and lettuce leaves, if using, and your favorite condiments.

MAKES 6 burgers

PORTOBELLO ALPINE BEEF BURGERS

Lean ground beef gets a flavor and nutrition boost from mushrooms and cheese.

1 portobello mushroom cap, stem and gills removed, finely chopped (about 1 cup)

1 cup (4 oz.) shredded Alpine Blend, Seriously Sharp, or Horseradish Cheddar

2 Tbsp. fine, dry breadcrumbs, preferably whole wheat

¾ tsp. table salt

½ tsp. garlic powder

1 lb. lean ground beef, 90% to 93% lean

1 tsp. extra virgin olive oil

4 buns, preferably whole grain, toasted, if desired

4 large slices tomato

Lettuce, sliced onion, reduced-fat mayonnaise, and pickle chips to serve, optional

COMBINE mushroom, cheese, breadcrumbs, salt, and garlic powder in a large bowl. Add beef, gently breaking up the meat and tossing with the cheese mixture. Gently press meat and cheese mixture together, kneading slightly. Form into 4 patties. Sprinkle with freshly ground black pepper to taste.

BRUSH oil over the bottom of a large nonstick pan, and place over medium heat. Add patties and cook until browned on bottoms, about 5 minutes. Turn gently, and continue cooking until burgers are cooked through and cheese is melting out the sides of the patties, about 5 minutes.

LET burgers rest 2 minutes before assembling on buns with tomato slices and lettuce, onion, mayonnaise, and pickle chips, if using.

MAKES 4 burgers

SPICY CHEDDAR BURGERS

½ lb. hot Italian turkey sausage,
    casings removed

½ lb. ground sirloin

1 cup (4 oz.) shredded Sharp Light
    Cheddar

½ tsp. chili powder

¼ tsp. ground chipotle chile pepper

¼ tsp. table salt

4 whole wheat buns

4 strips turkey bacon, cooked

Spinach, sliced tomatoes, and Chipotle
    Aïoli to serve, optional

A bouquet of spicy and smoky flavors brings this turkey and beef combo to the top of the heap. Don't forget to crown it with our light and kicky Chipotle Aïoli made with Greek-style yogurt.

PREHEAT grill to 300° to 350° (medium) heat. Combine sausage, sirloin, Cheddar, chili powder, ground chipotle chile pepper, and salt in a large bowl just until well blended. Shape into 4 patties. Place patties on grill, and cook 10 minutes per side or until cooked through.

TOAST buns on grill toward end of grilling time. Serve burgers topped with bacon, spinach, tomato, and Chipotle Aïoli (see below), if using.

MAKES 4 burgers

Chipotle Aïoli

¼ cup light mayonnaise

¼ cup plain Greek-style yogurt

2 Tbsp. Dijon mustard

1 Tbsp. white or cider vinegar

½ tsp. ground chipotle pepper or dash
    of chipotle hot sauce

WHISK together mayonnaise, yogurt, mustard, vinegar, and pepper or hot sauce in a small bowl. Serve immediately, or cover and refrigerate up to 2 weeks.

MAKES ⅔ cup

MARGARITA MARTINEZ'S MONTEREY JACK, GUAVA, AND ARUGULA SANDWICH

This sandwich is a more savory version of guava cheese pastries, a favorite treat in the Martinez household. Queso blanco, or white cheese, with guava is a common Puerto Rican snack.

2 oz. guava paste, cut into ¼-inch cubes

2 croissants, cut in half lengthwise

4 oz. Monterey Jack

1 cup loosely packed arugula, chopped

HEAT cubed guava paste and 2 Tbsp. water in a small saucepan set over medium-low heat. Cook, stirring frequently, 5 to 6 minutes or until a spreadable jam forms. Turn off heat and let sit in pan.

PREHEAT broiler. Place croissant halves, cut sides up, on a baking sheet. Toast 2 minutes or until lightly browned on the edges. Remove from oven and sprinkle each croissant half with 1 oz. cheese; broil 30 seconds or until cheese is melted but not browned.

SPREAD guava mixture evenly over top of cheese on all 4 croissant halves. Place ½ of chopped arugula on each of 2 croissant halves; top with remaining 2 croissant halves, guave mixture sides down. Cut each sandwich in half crosswise. Serve warm.

MAKES 2 sandwiches

 TIP>> Guava paste can be found in the Latin foods sections of most supermarkets.

CURRIED TURKEY WRAPS

½ cup plain Greek-style yogurt

¼ cup raisins

½ tsp. curry powder

4 spinach tortillas

1 cup (4 oz.) shredded Sharp
  Light Cheddar

6 oz. sliced turkey breast

1 cup baby spinach leaves

½ cup grated carrots

STIR together yogurt, raisins, and curry powder in a small bowl. Spread mixture over tortillas to within ½ inch of edge.

SPRINKLE each with ¼ cup Cheddar, followed by turkey breast, spinach leaves, and carrots.

ROLL tortillas up tightly, and wrap in plastic wrap. Refrigerate at least 1 hour before serving.

MAKES 4 wraps

These wraps are a simple but delicious way to change up the basic brown bag lunch sandwich. And unlike many sandwiches, they actually taste better when you make them the night before.

SWEET POTATO AND BLACK BEAN TORTILLA ROLLUPS

These healthy, cheesy tortilla rollups bring together the delicious flavors of sweet potato, black beans, and mild green chiles with taco seasoning.

1   small (6- to 8-oz.) sweet potato, peeled and cubed

1   (15-oz.) can black beans, drained and rinsed

½   cup fat-free cottage cheese

1   (4.5-oz.) can chopped green chiles, drained

1   Tbsp. taco seasoning

1   tsp. fresh lime juice

½   tsp. garlic powder

½   tsp. onion powder

½   cup (2 oz.) shredded Mozzarella

1   cup shredded cooked turkey or chicken, optional

3   Tbsp. chopped fresh cilantro

2   Tbsp. sliced green onions

8   (8-inch) high-fiber tortillas

¼   cup salsa

¼   cup plain Greek-style yogurt

PREHEAT oven to 425°. Line a baking sheet with aluminum foil, and coat lightly with cooking spray; set aside.

MICROWAVE sweet potato until tender, about 5 to 10 minutes. (Alternatively, cover with water in a small saucepan, bring to a simmer, and cook 5 to 10 minutes or until tender; drain.) Place sweet potato in a medium bowl, and mash. Stir in beans.

STIR together cottage cheese, chiles, taco seasoning, lime juice, garlic powder, and onion powder in another medium bowl. Stir in mozzarella and turkey or chicken, if using. Stir in sweet potato–bean mixture, cilantro, and green onions until well combined.

PLACE about one-eighth of filling on lower third of each tortilla, keeping it about ½ inch from edges, and roll up. (If using corn tortillas, first wrap 3 to 4 tortillas at a time in damp paper towels, and microwave for 20 to 30 seconds until soft and easy to roll.)

PLACE tortillas, seam sides down, in a single layer on prepared baking sheet; spray tops lightly with cooking spray to help them brown.

BAKE 12 to 15 minutes or until tortillas are crisp and golden on ends. Meanwhile, stir together salsa and yogurt for dipping sauce. Cool 5 to 10 minutes before serving.

MAKES 8 rollups

TIP>> For homemade taco seasoning, mix 1½ tsp. onion powder, 1½ tsp. chili powder, 1 tsp. ground cumin, 1 tsp. garlic powder, and 1 tsp. dried oregano.

Kalamata-Stuffed
Chicken with Creamy
Roasted Pepper Sauce,
page 165

the Family Table

LIGHT SUPPERS AND HEARTY MAINS

"We have a big table with many leaves.
There is always room to set more places."

—Theresa Freund, Freund's Farm,
East Canaan, Connecticut

BAKED MACARONI AND CHEDDAR

Everyone has a favorite mac-and-cheese recipe. This outstanding version has a crunchy bread-crumb topping and just a hint of zingy heat from a few (or several) dashes of hot sauce. It's a good base recipe to which you can add different types of Cheddar or other ingredients, just as each of our Cabot farm families does.

2¼ cups uncooked elbow macaroni

3 slices firm white or whole wheat bread, pulsed into crumbs in processor or blender

5 Tbsp. butter

3 cups milk

3 Tbsp. all-purpose flour

¾ tsp. table salt

¼ tsp. freshly ground black pepper

⅛ tsp. freshly grated nutmeg

Several dashes of hot sauce

1 (1-lb.) block sharp, extra sharp, or Smoky Bacon Cheddar, shredded and divided

PREHEAT oven to 375°. Butter a 13- x 9-inch or other shallow large baking dish.

BRING a large pot of salted water to a boil, and stir in macaroni. Return to a boil and cook, according to package directions, just until macaroni is cooked but still slightly firm. Immediately drain macaroni in a colander, and rinse under cold water; set aside.

PUT breadcrumbs in a small bowl. Put empty macaroni pot back over medium-low heat, and melt butter. Spoon 2 Tbsp. melted butter into breadcrumbs, and blend together thoroughly; set aside.

BRING milk just to a simmer in a medium saucepan set over medium-high heat. Lower heat; cover and keep warm.

RETURN pot with remaining melted butter to low heat, and whisk in flour until smooth. Cook 1 minute, whisking constantly. Gradually whisk in warm milk; cook over medium heat, whisking constantly, until mixture is thickened and bubbly.

REMOVE sauce from heat, and whisk in salt, pepper, nutmeg, hot sauce, and 2 cups Cheddar. Stir in macaroni.

SPREAD one-third of pasta mixture over bottom of prepared baking dish. Scatter one-third of remaining Cheddar on top. Spoon another one-third of pasta on top, and add another one-third of Cheddar. Top with remaining pasta. Mix remaining cheese into breadcrumbs, and scatter evenly over top.

BAKE 25 to 30 minutes or until golden on top and bubbling throughout. Let stand 10 minutes before serving.

MAKES 6 to 8 servings

TRY SOMETHING *different*

There are as many variations of this recipe as there are families who love macaroni and cheese. The Barstows of Longview Farm make a Pepper Jack Mac with half spicy Pepper Jack and half mild Cheddar. Lynn Poupore of PAPAS Dairy always stirs in her own homegrown canned tomatoes. Billie Jo of Krebs Organic Dairy Farm is famous for her mac and cheese, always made for a crowd. She starts with Seriously Sharp, adds Tomato Basil, Garlic & Herb, and Horseradish with smaller amounts of Alpine Cheddar, Habanero, and then, American to bring it all together.

MACARONI AND CHEESE WITH BUTTERNUT SQUASH

4 cups (about 1¼ lb.) cubed butternut squash

2 cups uncooked whole grain elbow macaroni

1 Tbsp. plus 1 tsp. canola oil, divided

2 shallots, minced

⅓ cup all-purpose flour

3 cups 1% low-fat milk

1 tsp. minced fresh rosemary

2 tsp. Dijon mustard

¾ tsp. table salt

¼ tsp. ground white pepper

1½ cups (6 oz.) shredded White Oak, sharp, or extra sharp Cheddar

3 Tbsp. whole wheat panko (Japanese breadcrumbs)

½ tsp. paprika

PREHEAT oven to 400°. Coat a 2- to 3-qt. baking dish with cooking spray.

BRING several inches of water to a boil in a large saucepan fitted with a steamer basket. Add squash and steam, covered, until very tender, 8 to 12 minutes. Mash about half of the squash in a small bowl, and set aside both mashed squash and remaining steamed cubes.

MEANWHILE, bring a large pot of salted water to a boil, and stir in macaroni. Return to a boil, and cook macaroni, according to package directions, just until it is cooked but still slightly firm. Immediately drain macaroni in a colander, and rinse under cold water; set aside.

PUT empty macaroni pot back over medium heat with 1 Tbsp. oil. Add shallots, and cook, stirring often, until softened and starting to turn golden, 1 to 3 minutes. Whisk in flour until blended. Cook 1 minute, whisking constantly. Gradually whisk in milk; cook over medium heat, whisking constantly, until mixture is thickened and bubbly. Whisk in rosemary, mustard, salt, and white pepper until smooth.

REMOVE from heat, and whisk in Cheddar. Add mashed squash, and whisk until combined. Stir in macaroni and squash cubes. Transfer to prepared baking dish.

MIX panko with remaining 1 tsp. oil and paprika in a small bowl until evenly moist and bright orange. Sprinkle over macaroni.

BAKE 15 to 20 minutes or until golden on top and bubbling throughout. Cool 10 minutes before serving.

MAKES 6 to 8 servings

Use whole grain macaroni and loads of sweet butternut squash to add a wholesome and very flavorful twist to macaroni and cheese, not to mention a sunny golden glow to the final dish.

GRACE POTTER'S MACARONI AND CHEDDAR "CUPCAKES"

Musician Grace Potter, a Vermont native, shares her love of Cheddar and macaroni and cheese with this fun spin, yielding personalized portions in a cupcake shape. She kicks it up with her signature white truffle oil and a variety of cheeses, including her spicy favorite, Hot Habanero. "These smell like heaven," Grace promises.

1   (14-oz.) box multigrain or whole wheat elbow macaroni

1   Tbsp. olive oil

1   small onion, diced

3   cloves garlic, minced

½   cup all-purpose flour

2   cups milk

1½   cups (6 oz.) shredded Seriously Sharp Cheddar

½   cup (2 oz.) shredded Hot Habanero Cheddar

1   cup (4 oz.) shredded Gruyère or other Swiss-style cheese

½   cup (2 oz.) finely grated Alpine Cheddar or Parmesan, divided

1   Tbsp. white truffle oil, optional

1   large egg

½   cup half-and-half

⅔   cup fine, dry cornbread stuffing mix or coarse, dry breadcrumbs

PREHEAT oven to 400°. Coat 18 cups of 2 (12-cup) muffin pans with cooking spray. Bring a large pot of salted water to a boil, and stir in macaroni. Return to a boil, and cook macaroni, according to package directions, just until cooked but still slightly firm. Immediately drain macaroni in a colander, and rinse under cold water; set aside.

HEAT 1 Tbsp. oil in a large skillet set over medium heat. Add onion and cook, stirring often, 2 to 3 minutes until softened. Add garlic and cook, stirring frequently, until fragrant and onion is just starting to turn golden. Whisk in flour until blended. Cook 1 minute, whisking constantly. Gradually whisk in milk; cook over medium heat, whisking constantly, until mixture is thickened and bubbly.

REMOVE from heat, and whisk in Cheddars and Gruyère. Stir in macaroni; stir in ¼ cup Alpine Cheddar or Parmesan and truffle oil, if using. Cool mixture 5 minutes. Add salt to taste.

MEANWHILE, beat egg and half-and-half together in a small bowl, and stir into cooled macaroni mixture. Divide mixture evenly among 18 prepared muffin cups.

MIX together cornbread stuffing mix or breadcrumbs and remaining ¼ cup Alpine Cheddar or Parmesan in a small bowl. Top each "cupcake" with crumb topping.

BAKE 15 to 20 minutes or until golden brown on top. Cool about 5 minutes before serving.

MAKES 18 large macaroni and cheese "cupcakes"

LIGHT MAC AND CHEESE

2   cups uncooked elbow macaroni, whole grain, optional

3   Tbsp. all-purpose flour

2   cups 1% low-fat milk

¼   tsp. dry mustard

¼   tsp. garlic powder, optional

¼   tsp. table salt

Pinch of ground red pepper

Dash of Worcestershire sauce

2   oz. Neufchâtel

2   cups (8 oz.) shredded Sharp Light Cheddar, divided

⅓   cup Italian-seasoned breadcrumbs or unseasoned dry breadcrumbs

PREHEAT oven to 350°. Coat a 2½-qt. baking dish with cooking spray.

BRING a large pot of salted water to a boil, and stir in macaroni. Return to a boil, and cook macaroni, according to package directions, just until cooked but still slightly firm. Immediately drain macaroni in a colander, and rinse under cold water; set aside.

PUT empty macaroni pot back over medium heat, and add flour; toast flour, stirring constantly until just golden. Gradually whisk in milk; cook over medium heat, whisking constantly, until mixture is thickened and bubbly, about 3 minutes. Whisk in mustard, garlic powder, if using, salt, red pepper, and Worcestershire sauce. Reduce heat to low. Stir in Neufchâtel until melted and well blended.

REMOVE from heat, and whisk in 1⅓ cups Cheddar. Stir in macaroni. Transfer to prepared baking dish.

MIX together breadcrumbs and remaining ⅔ cup Cheddar in a small bowl. Sprinkle over top of macaroni, and spray with cooking spray.

BAKE 20 minutes or until golden on top and bubbling throughout. Cool 10 minutes before serving.

MAKES 6 to 8 servings

When you're in the mood for mac and cheese but want something on the lighter side, try this version that delivers creamy taste and texture with a little less richness. Make it a one-pot meal by stirring in some thawed frozen broccoli florets or lightly steamed fresh broccoli.

GARGANELLI MAC AND CHEESE
WITH ROASTED JALAPEÑOS AND BACON

This flavor-packed macaroni and cheese was developed for Cabot by Joshua Rollins, the sous chef of The Pitcher Inn, a beautiful hotel in Vermont's Mad River Valley. Josh says he loves to combine sweet, smoky bacon with spicy jalapeño peppers. The tangy creaminess of Cheddar melds the two, creating a delicious combination.

2   jalapeño peppers

4   oz. (3 to 4 thick slices) applewood-smoked bacon, diced

¾   cup panko (Japanese breadcrumbs)

8   oz. (about 3 cups) uncooked garganelli or penne pasta

2   cups milk

2   Tbsp. butter

2   Tbsp. all-purpose flour

3   cups (12 oz.) shredded Clothbound, 3 Year, or Farmhouse Reserve Cheddar

PREHEAT broiler. Broil peppers on an aluminum foil–lined baking sheet 5 inches from heat 3 to 5 minutes on each side or until peppers look blistered. Place peppers in a zip-top plastic freezer bag; seal and let stand 10 minutes to loosen skins. Peel peppers; remove and discard seeds. Chop flesh into fine dice, and set aside.

REDUCE oven temperature to 350°. Lightly butter a 2-qt. baking dish or 4 to 6 ramekins. Cook bacon in a large skillet set over medium-high heat 6 to 8 minutes or until crisp; remove bacon with a slotted spoon to a small bowl. Add panko, along with a small amount of bacon fat to moisten, combining well; set aside.

BRING a large pot of salted water to a boil, and stir in pasta. Return to a boil, and cook pasta, according to package directions, just until cooked but still slightly firm. Immediately drain pasta in a colander, and rinse under cold water; set aside.

BRING milk just to a simmer in a medium saucepan set over medium-high heat. Lower heat; cover and keep warm. Melt butter in pot used for pasta set over medium heat, and whisk in flour until smooth. Cook 1 minute, whisking constantly. Gradually whisk in warm milk; cook over medium heat, whisking constantly, until mixture is thickened and bubbly.

REMOVE sauce from heat, and whisk in Cheddar. Stir in macaroni and reserved jalapeños. Add salt to taste. Transfer to prepared baking dish or ramekins, if using, and top with panko mixture. Bake 25 to 30 minutes or until golden on top and bubbling throughout. Cool 10 minutes before serving.

MAKES 4 to 6 servings

Laurel Brook Farm

EAST CANAAN, CONNECTICUT

LUNCH AT LAUREL BROOK FARM is a sacred thing. All four generations of the Jacquier family know to be at Robert and Dottie Jacquier's house each day for a home-cooked meal of spaghetti and meatballs, toasted cheese sandwiches and soup, or baked chicken and rice, always followed by ice cream and squash or apple pie, or, for special occasions, Dottie's famous ice-cream cake. "Ever since I can remember, my grandparents were adamant that we have lunch with them every day," says Cricket, who runs the farm with his brother, Bobby, and their dad, Peter. His grandmother adds, "Getting together every day always gave me a chance to ask questions." The fourth generation is represented by Bobby's two older sons, who also work on the farm; Cricket's wife, Jenn, does the books, in addition to working off-farm.

The farm has changed significantly since high-school sweethearts Robert and Dottie began farming with 12 cows in 1948. With 18 outside employees, 2,200 animals (including 1,050 milking head), 2,700 acres of cropland, and a robust business selling compost to landscapers, there is a lot to coordinate. But the standards they set remain strong. "My grandparents started out with nothing," Cricket says. "There were some very tough times. My grandfather lost a leg. There was the flood of 1955. They always believed in dairy and producing a good product. They taught us about always tying it back to the land, to the environment and the soil we deal with every day."

The Jacquier family has been involved as 4-H leaders for more than 60 years, and Cricket, like his grandfather did, serves on the co-op board of directors. "The challenge is to keep up with the technology, be willing and able to change, and know what drives your business," Cricket says. His cell phone chirps constantly (yes, like a cricket) with questions and issues. While growth of the business has been rewarding, Cricket notes that it comes with its own challenges. "A dairy farmer works every day from his heart," he says. Sundays, however, are his day to milk, something he considers critical. "There's nothing like being part of a daily routine that you're expecting others to do," he says.

Family, though, is the most valuable piece of the puzzle, from the noontime dinner tradition to keeping the next generation involved. "It's the whole family part of it— farming together and being able to make that work," Cricket says. He encourages his son and daughter to jump on the tractor with him when he heads down to the barn, and he takes hunting trips with them. "The memories I have of doing things with my dad," he says, "I want to make sure I don't miss those with my kids." Considering how he's made family a top priority, it's doubtful he will.

FARM FAMILY:
Dottie and Robert Jacquier with their son Peter, grandsons Cricket and Bobby and their families

YEARS OWNED:
67 [since 1948]

FARMSTEAD:
2,700 acres

HERD:
1,050 Holstein milking herd, total animals on-farm 2,200

OTHER FARM BUSINESS:
Compost

AWARDS:
Green Pastures Connecticut Dairy Farm of the Year 1974 and 2006, Dairy Farm of Distinction

Opposite page:
From left: Colby, Jenn, Morgan, Cricket, Jean, Pete, Robert, Dorothy, Bob, Teresa, Austin, Kayla (in front of Austin), Shelby, Dalton, and Bailey Jacquier

Laurel Brook Farm's BAKED CHICKEN AND RICE WITH MUSHROOMS AND CHEDDAR

Almost every day for more than half a century, farmer Dottie Jacquier has cooked up dinner for family members and visitors on their multi-generation farm. Her simple, hearty main courses include baked chicken with mushrooms, which inspired this recipe.

2	large leeks
¼	cup all-purpose flour
1	tsp. table salt
½	tsp. freshly ground black pepper
4	chicken leg quarters (3 lb.), cut into thighs and drumsticks
2	Tbsp. olive oil
12	oz. fresh mushrooms, quartered
1	tsp. fresh thyme leaves
1¼	cups uncooked long-grain rice, rinsed
2½	cups chicken stock
1	cup (4 oz.) shredded sharp Cheddar
¼	cup sour cream
3	Tbsp. butter
½	tsp. paprika

PREHEAT oven to 375°. Remove and discard root ends and dark green tops of leeks. Cut in half lengthwise, and rinse thoroughly under cold running water to remove grit and sand. Cut leeks crosswise into half-moon-shaped slices. Combine flour, salt, and pepper in a pie plate. Dredge chicken in flour mixture.

HEAT olive oil in a large ovenproof skillet set over medium-high heat. Cook chicken, in 2 batches, 4 minutes on each side or until browned; drain on paper towels, reserving 1 Tbsp. drippings in skillet.

SAUTÉ leeks, mushrooms, and thyme in hot drippings 5 minutes or until leeks are tender and mushrooms are lightly browned. Stir in rice; cook, stirring constantly, 2 minutes. Stir in chicken stock; bring to a boil. Add chicken; cover tightly, and bake 35 to 40 minutes or until liquid is absorbed and rice is tender.

REMOVE chicken pieces to a plate, and stir Cheddar and sour cream into rice. Replace chicken pieces on top of rice, dot with butter, sprinkle with paprika, and bake, uncovered, about 15 minutes or until chicken is browned and a meat thermometer inserted into thickest portion registers 165°.

MAKES 4 servings

GRILLED CHEESY PORTOBELLO CAPS WITH TURKEY AND SAGE

4   large portobello mushroom caps

1   tsp. extra virgin olive oil

1   shallot, minced

2   Tbsp. fine, dry breadcrumbs

4   tsp. minced fresh sage leaves

½   tsp. table salt

½   tsp. freshly ground black pepper

⅛   tsp. ground nutmeg

12   oz. lean ground turkey

¾   cup (3 oz.) shredded White Oak, sharp, or extra sharp Cheddar

Fresh sage leaves for garnish, optional

PREHEAT grill to 300° to 350° (medium) heat.

REMOVE stems from mushrooms. Using a spoon, scrape and discard brown gills from undersides of mushrooms, leaving edges of caps intact. Brush tops lightly with oil, and set aside on a platter, oiled sides down.

MIX together shallot, breadcrumbs, sage, salt, pepper, and nutmeg in a medium bowl. Add turkey and knead together just until seasonings are evenly distributed. Divide turkey mixture among mushroom caps.

PLACE mushrooms, filling sides up, on grill. Close lid (or cover with tent of aluminum foil), and cook 10 to 12 minutes or until turkey is cooked through to center.

TOP with Cheddar; cover and cook until Cheddar is melted, about 2 minutes. Garnish with fresh sage leaves, if using.

MAKES 4 servings

Large mushrooms provide a nice base for this quick and creative twist on a turkey burger with a hint of Thanksgiving flavor and a crown of melted sharp Cheddar. You can pop the stuffed mushrooms on the grill during warm weather or use the oven.

TRY SOMETHING *different*

To make these in the oven, first broil mushroom caps on a rimmed baking sheet 3 to 5 minutes or until just tender. Reduce heat to 400°, and bake filled mushrooms on middle rack of oven about 15 minutes or until turkey is cooked through. Top with Cheddar, set oven back to broil, and broil 2 minutes or until Cheddar is melted.

ROASTED CHICKEN SAUSAGE WITH POTATOES AND APPLES

This easy, hearty meal for a chilly fall or winter day combines savory with a little sweet, all deliciously caramelized in a hot oven. Add a crisp green salad or steamed green beans, and dinner is served.

1½ lb. baby potatoes, such as red, blue, or gold, cut into 1-inch chunks (about 6 cups)

1   Tbsp. extra virgin olive oil

1   tsp. kosher salt

½   tsp. freshly ground black pepper

4   (12-oz.) fully cooked chicken sausages, sliced

2   sweet, juicy apples, such as Golden Delicious, cut into 1-inch chunks

2   Tbsp. whole grain mustard

2   Tbsp. honey

1   Tbsp. cider vinegar or red wine vinegar

1   cup (4 oz.) shredded Alpine Cheddar, Seriously Sharp, or extra sharp Cheddar

Parsley, optional

PREHEAT oven to 450°. Toss potatoes, oil, salt, and pepper in a large bowl until coated. Spread out in a large heavy roasting pan. Roast 20 minutes, stirring once or twice.

MEANWHILE, stir sausage, apple, mustard, honey, and vinegar together in the same bowl.

REDUCE oven temperature to 375°. Remove roasting pan from oven. Scrape potatoes up from the pan with a spatula. Add sausage mixture to potatoes, and toss to combine. Return pan to oven, and bake, stirring once or twice, 30 to 35 minutes or until potatoes and apples are tender and glaze is caramelized.

SCRAPE potato mixture into center of roasting pan. Top with Cheddar, and return to oven 2 to 3 minutes or just until cheese is melted. Garnish with parsley, if using, and serve immediately.

MAKES 6 servings

KALAMATA-STUFFED CHICKEN
WITH CREAMY ROASTED PEPPER SAUCE

6   skinned and boned chicken breasts

¾   tsp. table salt, divided

½   tsp. freshly ground black pepper

½   cup (2 oz.) shredded sharp Cheddar

½   cup finely chopped kalamata olives

½   cup Italian-seasoned breadcrumbs

1   (7-oz.) jar roasted red bell peppers, drained and patted dry

½   cup plain Greek-style yogurt

Mixed salad greens to serve, optional

PREHEAT oven to 350°. Coat an 11- x 9-inch baking dish with cooking spray.

PLACE chicken breasts between 2 sheets of heavy-duty plastic wrap, and flatten to ¼-inch thickness, using a rolling pin or flat side of a meat mallet. Season with ½ tsp. salt and pepper.

SPRINKLE Cheddar and olives evenly onto center of each chicken breast; roll up, jelly-roll fashion, and secure with wooden picks. Dredge chicken rolls in breadcrumbs.

PLACE rolls, seam sides down, in prepared baking dish, and lightly coat rolls with cooking spray. Bake 25 to 30 minutes or until chicken is cooked through to center.

MEANWHILE, pulse red bell peppers in food processor until pureed; add yogurt and remaining ¼ tsp. salt, pulsing just until smooth. Refrigerate until ready to serve.

REMOVE chicken from oven, and remove wooden picks. Cool slightly. Slice breasts crosswise into 1-inch-thick slices; arrange over salad greens, if using, and serve drizzled with red bell pepper sauce.

MAKES 6 servings

This beautiful presentation is elegant enough for company yet simple enough for a weeknight family dinner. A bowl of rice pilaf or steamed couscous rounds out the meal.

BEER-MARINATED PORK TENDERLOIN WITH CHARRED CORN-CHEDDAR RELISH

Start the pork marinating the morning before you plan to serve this impressive yet easy dish, which features a colorful relish bursting with flavor.

Pork

1   (12-oz.) bottle amber ale
½   cup pure maple syrup
¼   cup fresh lime juice
2   Tbsp. olive oil
1   Tbsp. Dijon mustard
3   cloves garlic, minced
1   tsp. kosher salt
½   tsp. freshly ground black pepper
2   (1- to 1½-lb.) pork tenderloins

Relish

1½ cups fresh corn kernels (or frozen corn kernels, thawed)
½   cup finely diced jarred roasted red bell peppers
½   cup (2 oz.) finely diced sharp Cheddar
¼   cup chopped fresh cilantro or parsley
2   Tbsp. olive oil
1   Tbsp. fresh lime juice
¼   tsp. table salt
⅛   tsp. freshly ground black pepper

MARINATE PORK: Whisk together ale, syrup, lime juice, oil, mustard, garlic, salt, and pepper in a bowl, and pour into a large zip-top plastic freezer bag; add pork, turning to coat. Seal and chill at least 8 hours but not more than 12 hours.

PREPARE RELISH: Place a large nonstick or cast-iron skillet over high heat. When skillet is hot, add corn and cook, stirring occasionally, until corn is nicely browned, about 3 to 5 minutes. (Be prepared for some kernels to pop out of the skillet.) Transfer corn to a medium bowl. When cool, add bell peppers, Cheddar, cilantro or parsley, oil, lime juice, salt, and black pepper; combine well. Refrigerate until ready to serve.

REMOVE tenderloins from marinade, shaking off and discarding excess. Preheat one side of gas grill or prepare coals on one side of charcoal grill to 400° to 450° (high) heat. When hot, place tenderloins directly over heat, and cook, turning until browned on all sides, 2 to 3 minutes per side.

TRANSFER tenderloins to indirect portion of grill; close lid of grill or tent with heavy-duty aluminum foil or inverted foil roasting pan, and continue cooking until only slightly pink in center and a meat thermometer inserted in thickest portion registers 145°, 3 to 5 minutes longer. Remove from grill, and let rest 5 minutes for juices to settle. Cut tenderloin into thick slices, and serve with relish.

MAKES 6 to 8 servings

KITCHEN WISDOM

The pork makes a great centerpiece for a special family or neighborhood barbecue, and it can also be made in the oven.

EARLY IN THEIR RELATIONSHIP, Joanna and Adam Lidback bonded over their appreciation of cows. Joanna knew things were getting serious when Adam offered to care for her Jersey cows along with his herd of Holsteins. "The heifers went there first and then my milk cows," Joanna recalls. "Then we got our first dog together, and she went up there. Then, in 2010, we got married."

Though neither one was raised on a farm, it's a natural fit. Growing up, Adam found himself drawn to his mother's family's farm, spending every summer there. "I love working the land. I always thought I'd farm," he says. He studied animal science, worked for a builder, and then eventually came to work full time at the family farm in 2008.

Joanna was very involved with 4-H as a youngster living in rural Massachusetts. "I fell in love with the animals. I couldn't wait for the day that I could have my own calf," she recalls. She pursued studies in agriculture and business and planned to work for an international antihunger organization. Then, she says, "I realized there's plenty of work to be done here."

Adam's aunt and uncle, David and Juliette Stevens, have conserved the farmland and continue to help as the Lidbacks establish themselves. The barn is set up to milk 100 cows, and the young couple are building their herd, "a mix of Holsteins and Jerseys," says Adam. "Jerseys and Holsteins," corrects Joanna with a grin. The family sells hay

The Farm at Wheeler Mountain

BARTON, VERMONT

and pasture-raised, grass-fed Jersey beef. Joanna does the books and also works full time from home as an agriculture research consultant. She still likes to get down to the barn to do chores when she can. "Sometimes, after our two sons are asleep in the late evening, if we have a cow close to calving," Joanna says, "I'll go down and check on her. In the barn, it's so peaceful. The cows are calm, lying down, and they look at you like, 'What are you doing here?'"

Both the Lidbacks love when days get longer and the animals head out to pasture. "The cows get spring fever. They really kind of kick up their heels," says Joanna. Warm weather also makes it easier to take the kids down to the barn to see the animals and visit their dad. Their older son figured out how to feed the cows by the time he was 2, Joanna says proudly: "He'd grab a scoop and fill it with calf grain and then head out to the heifers."

"So often Adam and I look at each other and say, 'How did we get here?'" Joanna marvels. "But I think that we're here for a reason, and we're trying to make the most of it. It's a much different industry than it was for the generation that came before us, certainly the generation before that. We talk a lot about sustainability and what that means, but it all comes down to making the farm available, useful, and resourceful for the next generation. That we might be looking in their faces (of the next generation) every day is pretty exciting."

FARM FAMILY:
Adam and Joanna Lidback

FARMSTEAD:
250 acres

HERD:
Total of 100 Holsteins and Jerseys, milking 50

OTHER FARM BUSINESS:
Grass-fed Jersey beef, hay, compost

AWARDS:
Top regional producer quality award from Lancaster Dairy Herd Improvement Association 2012

The Farm at Wheeler Mountain's
ZUCCHINI BEEF BOATS

2   medium (12 to 14 oz. each) zucchini

Butter

1   lb. lean ground beef

1   cup chopped red bell pepper

⅔   cup chopped onion

3   Tbsp. ketchup

1   Tbsp. Worcestershire sauce

1   tsp. table salt

½   tsp. freshly ground black pepper

1   cup (4 oz.) shredded mild or sharp Cheddar, divided

PREHEAT oven to 350°. Slice zucchini in half lengthwise and create cavities by scooping out centers of zucchini halves, leaving ½-inch-thick shells. Coarsely chop zucchini pulp. Place shells in a buttered 13- x 9-inch baking dish.

BROWN ground beef in a large skillet set over medium-high heat, stirring often, 7 to 9 minutes or until meat crumbles and is no longer pink. Remove beef from skillet with a slotted spoon, reserving drippings in skillet. Cook bell pepper, onion, and zucchini pulp in hot drippings, stirring occasionally, 10 minutes or until tender and golden. Remove from heat.

STIR in beef, ketchup, Worcestershire sauce, salt, pepper, and ½ cup Cheddar. Spoon filling evenly into zucchini shells. Pour ½ cup water around zucchini shells.

COVER and bake 35 to 40 minutes or until zucchini is tender. Uncover and sprinkle with remaining ½ cup Cheddar. Increase heat to 375°, and bake 10 more minutes or until cheese is browned.

MAKES 4 servings

Filling her garden-grown zucchini with a mixture that includes some of the farm's own Jersey beef and a little Cheddar is just one of the creative ways that busy mom and farmer Joanna Lidback gets her young sons to eat their vegetables.

SPINACH, CHEESE, AND HAM CANNELLONI

This quick version of Italian cannelloni—made with rolled, stuffed lasagna noodles—is a snap to make and pretty enough to serve to company. Serve over additional steamed spinach with garlic bread.

10 "no-boil" lasagna noodles

1 large egg

2 cups cottage cheese

1¼ cups (5 oz.) shredded Tomato Basil or mild Cheddar, divided

½ cup cooked chopped fresh or frozen spinach, squeezed dry (about 5 oz. fresh spinach)

½ cup (2 oz.) finely chopped ham

¾ cup marinara sauce, divided

PREHEAT oven to 350°. Fill a large bowl with very hot tap water; add noodles, separating them from each other as much as possible, and let stand 10 minutes or until softened.

MEANWHILE, whisk egg until frothy in a medium bowl. Stir in cottage cheese, 1 cup Cheddar, spinach, and ham.

SPREAD ¼ cup marinara sauce over bottom of a 13- x 9-inch baking dish.

REMOVE noodles from water, blot dry, and place on work surface. Place about ¼ cup filling across one short end of each, and roll up. Place cannelloni on top of sauce in baking dish. Arrange into two lengthwise, slightly separated rows. Spoon remaining ½ cup marinara sauce over top. Sprinkle evenly with remaining ¼ cup Cheddar. Cover dish tightly with aluminum foil.

BAKE 40 to 45 minutes or until sauce is bubbling and most juices have been absorbed. Remove from oven, and let stand, covered, about 5 minutes.

MAKES 5 servings

EASY ARTICHOKE PIZZA POCKET

1   lb. homemade or store-bought
    pizza dough

2   cups (8 oz.) shredded Sharp Light
    Cheddar or mozzarella

1   cup sliced canned artichoke hearts

½   cup julienned sun-dried tomatoes,
    drained of oil

1   cup loosely packed roughly chopped
    fresh basil leaves

2   slices cooked crumbled bacon,
    optional

PREHEAT oven to 425°. Line a baking sheet with parchment paper. Pat or roll pizza dough into a 15- x 10-inch rectangle directly on prepared baking sheet.

SPRINKLE cheese lengthwise down center of dough, leaving about a 2½-inch border on each side. Layer artichoke hearts, tomatoes, basil, and bacon, if using, evenly over cheese.

MAKE 14 to 15 diagonal cuts, each 2 inches long and about 1 inch apart, on opposite sides of dough to within ½ inch of filling, using a sharp knife or kitchen shears. Pull strips over filling, crisscrossing strips diagonally. Press ends under to seal.

BAKE 15 minutes or until golden brown. Let stand 5 minutes. Cut crosswise into slices.

MAKES 4 servings

ROASTED VEGETABLE TART
WITH CHEDDAR-CORNMEAL CRUST

1   cup plain or stone-ground yellow cornmeal

2   cups (8 oz.) shredded Sharp Light Cheddar, divided

1   tsp. sugar

½   tsp. kosher salt

1   large egg

⅓   cup 2% reduced-fat milk

2½ Tbsp. olive oil, divided

3   small tomatoes, sliced

1   bunch green onions, trimmed and halved lengthwise

2   portobello mushrooms, stems and gills removed, sliced

1   medium-size red bell pepper, seeded and cut into strips

About 8 delicate mushrooms, such as enoki or oyster, torn into thin strips

2   Tbsp. finely shredded Alpine Cheddar or Parmesan

PREHEAT oven to 400°. Coat an 11-inch tart pan with cooking spray.

STIR together cornmeal, 1 cup shredded Cheddar, sugar, and salt in a medium bowl. Whisk egg until frothy in another bowl; then whisk in milk and 1½ Tbsp. oil. Stir milk mixture into dry ingredients until well blended.

PRESS crust mixture over bottom and slightly up sides of tart pan. Bake crust 14 to 16 minutes or until lightly browned. Cool on a wire rack.

LINE a large rimmed baking sheet with parchment paper. Arrange tomatoes, green onions, portobellos, and bell pepper on sheet, and drizzle with remaining 1 Tbsp. oil. Season with salt and pepper to taste. Roast vegetables 15 minutes or until just tender; cool slightly.

LAYER portobello mushrooms in crust; top with bell pepper strips. Sprinkle with ½ cup of remaining Cheddar. Add a layer of green onions and then a layer of tomato slices. Sprinkle with remaining ½ cup Cheddar. Arrange enoki or oyster mushrooms on top, and sprinkle with Alpine Cheddar or Parmesan.

BAKE tart 20 minutes or until lightly browned on top.

MAKES 6 to 8 servings

This beautiful tart makes a gorgeous centerpiece for a vegetarian meal or a contribution to a buffet or potluck. You can switch up the vegetables, depending on what's fresh at the market; roasting them really brings out their flavor.

INDIVIDUAL CHILI-CHEDDAR MEATLOAVES

These adorable meatloaves pack a spicy punch thanks to chili sauce and powder, along with Jalapeño Cheddar.

1   small onion, chopped

½   green bell pepper, chopped

2   small garlic cloves, minced

½   cup chili sauce or ketchup, divided

3   cups (12 oz.) shredded Jalapeño Light Cheddar, divided

12   oz. extra-lean ground beef

2   Tbsp. pure maple syrup

2   tsp. chili powder

12   crushed saltine crackers

½   tsp. freshly ground black pepper

Dash or two of Worcestershire sauce

¼   tsp. dried crushed red pepper

2   large eggs, lightly beaten

¼   tsp. table salt

PREHEAT oven to 350°. Coat 8 muffin cups with cooking spray. Coat a large nonstick skillet with cooking spray, and place over medium heat. Add onion, bell pepper, and garlic; cook, stirring occasionally, 3 to 5 minutes or until tender. Combine onion mixture, ¼ cup chili sauce, 1 cup Cheddar, ground beef, maple syrup, chili powder, saltine crackers, black pepper, Worcestershire sauce, crushed red pepper, beaten eggs, and salt in a medium bowl.

SPOON meat mixture into muffin cups. Top with remaining 2 cups Cheddar.

BAKE 12 minutes. Top with remaining ¼ cup chili sauce. Bake 10 more minutes or until a meat thermometer inserted into center registers 160°. Let stand 5 minutes before serving.

MAKES 4 servings

KITCHEN WISDOM Don't be tempted to use a higher fat ground beef. Using the leanest meat available helps ensure the right texture in this meatloaf since the juices are trapped and can't drain away during cooking.

Wheeler Farm's
SUMMER SQUASH AND SAUSAGE CASSEROLE

1 lb. ground pork or turkey sausage

¾ cup finely diced onion

½ tsp. table salt

1½ lb. yellow squash or zucchini, sliced

2 large eggs

2 Tbsp. butter, melted

½ cup fine, dry breadcrumbs

1 cup (4 oz.) shredded Seriously Sharp Cheddar

PREHEAT oven to 350°. Lightly grease an 8-inch square baking dish with cooking spray.

BROWN sausage in a large skillet set over medium-high heat, stirring often, 7 to 9 minutes or until meat crumbles and is no longer pink. Transfer sausage to a large bowl with a slotted spoon. Reserve 1 Tbsp. drippings in skillet. Add onion and salt to hot drippings; sauté 4 minutes or until tender. Add squash and cook 9 minutes or until lightly browned, stirring occasionally. Add ¼ cup water. Cover and cook 5 minutes or until squash is tender. Cool slightly in skillet.

WHISK eggs, butter, and breadcrumbs together in a small bowl. Season with pepper. Stir sausage and egg mixture gently into squash. Spoon into prepared dish. Sprinkle Cheddar over top.

BAKE 25 minutes or until bubbly and brown. Let stand 5 minutes before serving.

MAKES 6 servings

The farmstand at Wheeler Farm (*see profile on page 37*) bursts with bright, fresh vegetables every summer and fall thanks to Karen Wheeler's fine gardening skills. August always brings a bumper harvest of yellow summer squash and zucchini. Although her husband, Rob, admits squash is not his favorite vegetable, he is a big fan of this casserole.

DOUBLE-BAKED CORNED BEEF POTATOES

Double-baked potatoes are always a crowd-pleaser, and this version is perfect for St. Patty's Day or any other day you feel like serving it up. A crunchy slaw with a tangy and light Greek-style yogurt dressing goes well with this dish *(see dressing for Broccoli Salad with Cheddar, Fennel, and Bacon, page 204).*

6	medium baking potatoes	2	Tbsp. minced fresh chives
1	Tbsp. vegetable oil	2	Tbsp. milk
½	cup sour cream	1	Tbsp. ketchup
⅓	cup chopped corned beef	1	Tbsp. sweet pickle relish
¼	cup (1 oz.) shredded Sharp Light Cheddar		

PREHEAT oven to 400°. Rub potatoes with oil, and place on a baking sheet. Bake 1 hour or until tender when pierced with a knife.

WHEN cool enough to handle (but not completely cool), slice off tops lengthwise. Scoop out flesh into a medium bowl, leaving shells intact.

MASH potatoes in a large bowl. Add sour cream, corned beef, Cheddar, chives, milk, ketchup, and relish; combine thoroughly. Season with salt and pepper to taste.

SPOON mixture into potato shells, and place on baking sheet. Bake about 15 minutes or until heated through.

MAKES 6 servings

Farmer Alison Kosakowski Conant (*see profile on page 236*) is as proud of her Polish roots as she is of her fancifully tufted Polish chickens. She combined her classic potato dumplings known as pierogi, with added dairy— Cheddar, sour cream, and cottage cheese.

Conant's Riverside Farms'
CHEDDAR PIEROGI

Dough

½ cup sour cream

¼ tsp. table salt

2 large eggs

2 cups all-purpose flour, plus more for dusting

Filling

1 (8-oz.) baking potato, peeled and cut into 1½-inch cubes

½ cup cottage cheese

½ cup (2 oz.) extra sharp Cheddar

¼ cup finely minced onion

1 Tbsp. sour cream

½ tsp. garlic powder

¼ tsp. freshly ground black pepper

⅛ tsp. table salt

Fried onions, sour cream to serve, optional

PREPARE DOUGH: Beat ½ cup sour cream, ¼ tsp. salt, and eggs at medium-low speed with a heavy-duty electric stand mixer using paddle attachment until blended. Gradually add flour, beating 3 to 4 minutes or until a dough forms. (Dough will be sticky.)

KITCHEN WISDOM To freeze: Place uncooked pierogi on a wax paper–lined baking sheet; freeze until firm. Transfer to a zip-top plastic freezer bag, and store in freezer up to 1 month. Do not thaw before cooking.

TURN dough out onto a floured surface, and knead 1 to 2 minutes to form a soft dough. Divide dough into 2 equal pieces. Wrap each piece in plastic wrap, and let rest 30 minutes.

MEANWHILE, PREPARE FILLING: Cook potato in boiling salted water to cover 10 minutes or until tender; drain well. Combine potato, cottage cheese, Cheddar, onion, 1 Tbsp. sour cream, garlic powder, pepper, and ⅛ tsp. salt in a medium bowl with a potato masher until blended.

UNWRAP 1 piece of dough, and roll to ⅛-inch thickness on a lightly floured work surface. Cut into 18 circles with a 2½-inch round cutter, rerolling dough once; place circles on a baking sheet dusted with flour. Repeat procedure with remaining piece of dough. Place about 1 tsp. filling in center of each circle (there will be some leftover filling). Brush edges of circles with water. Fold dough over filling, and crimp edges with a fork to seal. Cook pierogi, in 2 batches, in boiling salted water in a large Dutch oven 2 minutes or until they begin to float. Remove from water with a slotted spoon. After they are removed from boiling water, pierogi may be browned in melted butter before serving. Serve hot with fried onions and sour cream, if using.

MAKES 3 dozen

FISH TACOS WITH YOGURT CREMA AND MANDARIN-AVOCADO SALSA

1   (11-oz.) can mandarin oranges, drained

1   avocado, diced

1   tsp. chili powder

¾   cup plain Greek-style yogurt

1   Tbsp. fresh lime juice

2   tsp. ground cumin

1½ cups shredded red or green cabbage

1   cup (4 oz.) shredded Pepper Jack Light, Jalapeño Light, Chipotle, or Hot Habanero Cheddar

8   (6-inch) corn tortillas

¾   lb. cooked white fish, such as cod or tilapia

COMBINE mandarin oranges, avocado, and chili powder in a small serving bowl, and toss gently to combine. Stir together yogurt, lime juice, and cumin in another small serving bowl. Add salt to taste. Place cabbage and shredded cheese in two more small bowls.

TOAST tortillas directly on gas or electric stove burner heated to high, turning with tongs as tortillas become lightly charred on both sides; stack on a plate, and cover to keep warm. (Alternatively, toast tortillas in a dry skillet set over medium-high heat.)

IF USING leftover cooked fish, cover and microwave just until heated through, about 1 minute.

DIVIDE fish evenly between tortillas, and top with cheese, salsa, yogurt crema, and cabbage.

MAKES 4 servings

 TIP>> If cooking fish specifically for this recipe, place raw fillets in a baking dish lightly coated with oil. Sprinkle fish with a little ground cumin, chili powder, and salt. Bake at 350° for 15 to 20 minutes depending on thickness of fish, just until fish flakes easily with a fork.

These delicious and healthy tropical tacos are a great way to use up cooked fish leftovers, or you can cook fish just to make the meal. Black Bean and Rainbow Pepper Salad (*see page 204*) makes a healthy complement.

QUICK YOGURT-CURRIED SHRIMP

½ cup plain Greek-style yogurt

2 Tbsp. chopped fresh cilantro

2 tsp. minced fresh ginger

2 tsp. minced garlic

1 tsp. ground cumin

½ tsp. curry powder

¼ tsp. kosher salt

1 to 1 ¼ lb. (about 24) peeled medium-size raw shrimp

1 Tbsp. canola oil

½ lemon, optional

WHISK together yogurt, cilantro, ginger, garlic, cumin, curry powder, and salt in a medium bowl. Mix in shrimp to coat well; cover and refrigerate 30 to 60 minutes.

HEAT oil in large nonstick skillet set over medium-high heat. Remove shrimp from marinade, and add to skillet. Cook, stirring frequently, about 3 minutes or until opaque in center.

TRANSFER to plates, and serve topped with a squeeze of lemon juice, if using.

MAKES 4 servings

TRY SOMETHING *different*

This versatile marinade marries well with chicken, lamb, and even fish. You can use it to marinate cubes of chicken or lamb, and then grill or broil them. Spread it on top of fish fillets, and then bake them at 350° for about 15 to 20 minutes or just until fish flakes easily with a fork, depending on thickness of fish.

The Indian-inspired marinade used in this shrimp dish has been a favorite of Pat Richardson, of Richardson Family Farm (*see profile on page 231*), ever since she first pulled it from a Cabot brochure years ago. Serve it over steamed basmati rice with some quick sautéed green beans.

SIMPLE SALMON CAKES
WITH GREEK-STYLE YOGURT

Customize basic
salmon cakes
by adding your
favorite seafood
seasoning like
chopped capers,
minced green
onions, or fresh
herbs like basil
or thyme. The
Greek-style yogurt
holds the mixture
together nicely and
keeps the salmon
cakes moist. Serve
them on a bed
of greens with
Rotini and Pepper
Jack Salad with
Lemon Vinaigrette
(*see page 218*).

6   oz. cooked salmon, broken up,
    or 8 oz. raw salmon, finely diced

¼   cup 2% reduced-fat plain Greek-style
    yogurt

2   Tbsp. panko (Japanese breadcrumbs)

1   tsp. Dijon mustard

¼   tsp. kosher salt

¼   tsp. freshly ground black pepper

1   Tbsp. butter

MIX together salmon, yogurt, panko, mustard, salt, pepper, and any additional season-ings in a medium bowl. With moistened hands, form mixture into 4 round, flat patties. Refrigerate about 30 minutes.

MELT butter in a nonstick skillet set over medium heat. Add salmon cakes, and cook 3 to 4 minutes or until nicely browned on each side.

MAKES 2 servings

Freund's Farm's
Sweet Corn
Pudding, page 190

Peak Harvest

VEGETABLES, SALADS, AND SIDE DISHES

"Summer means the smell of fresh-cut hay
and an overflowing garden. I always can
about 250 quarts of tomatoes. Our kids
come home for my canned tomatoes."

—Lynn Poupore, PAPAS Dairy,
Malone, New York

Freund's Farm's SWEET CORN PUDDING

½ cup all-purpose flour

½ cup yellow cornmeal

2 Tbsp. sugar

1 Tbsp. baking powder

½ tsp. table salt

3 large eggs

1½ cups sour cream

6 Tbsp. unsalted butter, melted

3½ cups fresh corn kernels (from about 7 ears of corn) or frozen whole kernel corn, thawed

½ cup minced seeded jalapeño pepper (about 3 peppers), optional

PREHEAT oven to 350°. Lightly grease a 13- x 9-inch baking dish with cooking spray. Combine flour, cornmeal, sugar, baking powder, and salt in a medium bowl; make a well in center of mixture.

WHISK eggs in a large bowl. Whisk in sour cream and melted butter; add to dry mixture, stirring just until moistened. Stir in corn and, if using, jalapeños. Pour batter into prepared dish.

BAKE 30 minutes or until center is set.

MAKES 8 to 10 servings

Many Cabot farmers grow sweet corn and make their own version of this traditional recipe. Theresa Freund's *(see profile on page 127)* dish is softer, moister, and closer to pudding than cornbread; her girls like it with diced jalapeños stirred in.

KITCHEN WISDOM

When you work with hot peppers, wear gloves or, if you are using your bare hands, take great care not to touch your eyes without washing your hands thoroughly.

TIP>> You can use ¾ cup plain Greek-style yogurt in place of the same amount of sour cream for a slightly lighter result.

See "Kitchen Wisdom" on page 94 for a tip on removing kernels easily from fresh corn.

BAKED CAULI-NUGGETS

¾ lb. (about half a head) cauliflower

1 large egg

1 cup (4 oz.) shredded Sharp Light Cheddar

¼ cup fine cornmeal

1 tsp. kosher salt

A few grinds of black pepper

½ tsp. dry mustard

PREHEAT oven to 400°. Coat 2 (12-cup) mini-muffin pans with cooking spray.

COARSELY shred cauliflower with the shredding disc of a food processor or the coarse holes of a grater. (You should have about 3 cups.) Transfer to a clean kitchen towel, and squeeze out excess moisture.

BEAT egg lightly in a large bowl; stir in shredded cauliflower, Cheddar, cornmeal, salt, pepper, and mustard until well blended.

DIVIDE mixture evenly among muffin cups, and press down firmly. Bake 15 to 20 minutes or until golden brown.

MAKES 24 nuggets

TIP>> Any extras can be refrigerated for a few days and rewarmed in a low oven on a baking sheet loosely covered with aluminum foil.

A genius, sneaky way to get kids (and others who should know better) to eat their vegetables, these little cheesy, crispy, bite-size nuggets are sure to be a crowd-pleaser.

CHEDDAR GREEN BEAN CASSEROLE

This from-scratch version of the classic holiday green bean casserole combines fresh flavors with the traditional creaminess and crunch.

1½ lb. green beans, trimmed and cut into 1-inch pieces (about 6 cups)

1 Tbsp. butter

4½ tsp. extra virgin olive oil, divided

3 shallots, minced

8 oz. cremini or white mushrooms, finely chopped

2 tsp. minced fresh thyme

½ tsp. table salt

¼ tsp. freshly ground black pepper

¼ cup dry sherry

⅓ cup all-purpose flour

1 cup reduced-sodium chicken or vegetable broth

1 cup 1% low-fat milk

2 cups (8 oz.) shredded Seriously Sharp Cheddar

3 Tbsp. fine, dry breadcrumbs

½ tsp. paprika

¼ tsp. onion powder

Sprig of fresh thyme for garnish, optional

PREHEAT oven to 425°. Coat a 2-qt. baking dish with cooking spray. Bring several inches of water to a boil in a large saucepan fitted with a steamer basket. Add green beans and steam until crisp-tender, about 4 minutes. Carefully remove steamer basket from saucepan to stop beans from cooking further.

HEAT butter and 4 tsp. oil in a large skillet set over medium-high heat. Add shallots and cook 2 to 3 minutes or until just starting to brown. Add mushrooms, thyme, salt, and pepper, and cook, stirring occasionally, 3 to 4 minutes or until mushrooms have released their juices and liquid has evaporated. Add sherry and cook, stirring occasionally, 2 to 3 minutes or until liquid has evaporated.

SPRINKLE flour over mushroom mixture and stir to coat. Add broth and milk, and bring to a simmer, stirring often, about 5 minutes or until sauce is thickened.

REMOVE skillet from heat, and stir in 1½ cups Cheddar. Add green beans, and stir to combine. Transfer to prepared dish. Top with remaining ½ cup Cheddar.

STIR together breadcrumbs and remaining ½ tsp. oil in a small bowl. Add paprika and onion powder, and stir until breadcrumbs are evenly moist and bright orange. Sprinkle over casserole.

BAKE 20 to 25 minutes or until bubbling and golden brown on top. Let cool about 15 minutes before serving. Garnish with fresh thyme, if using.

MAKES 10 servings

PAPAS Dairy

MALONE, NEW YORK

From left: Alan Poupore, Aaron's son Wally Poupore and Aaron Poupore

NO SMOKING

ERIKA POUPORE HAS WARM MEMORIES of growing up within the embrace of her large family. The second youngest of Alan and Lynn Poupore's six grown children, she remembers summer barbecues and holidays that drew dozens of cousins, off-spring of her dad's seven siblings, including the four brothers with whom he went into business. It was 1998 when they consolidated their individual farms into PAPAS Dairy. The name honors their late father ("Papa" in the family's French-Canadian heritage) and stands for the initials of the brothers' names: Peter, Alan, Patrick, Aaron, and Scott. Sadly, Patrick died in an accident, but the remaining four brothers have now been joined by three members of the next generation.

Despite PAPAS's relatively large size among Northeastern dairies, the Poupore brothers are involved in every aspect of cropping 4,000 acres and caring for over 2,000 milking cows and about the same number of young stock. Grandma Poupore still lives in the white farmhouse on the home farm, and two of Erika's sisters work for Cabot in Vermont.

Commitment to farming was never a question for previous generations. As Lynn recounts it, her father-in-law and two of his brothers turned down the opportunity to try out for professional baseball teams to stay on the farm. "That's a love of farming right there," she says. Alan remembers doing chores before he was school age and then not wanting to leave for school. "He was driving the tractor with his brothers when they were so small that one had to work the pedal while the other held the steering wheel," says Lynn, who is a teacher.

Although Alan still gets up five days a week at 4:30 a.m. (and 3:30 a.m. on Sundays), consolidating the brothers' five farms helps spread responsibility and allows each to take time off when needed. "We can cover for each other easier," Alan says. "And we get along pretty good. Always have." In the fall, having coverage he can trust means a little bit of hunting, and in early spring, a warm-weather vacation with his wife. Other than that, he's happy working with the cows.

Getting up early doesn't bother him. "I like spring mornings because you can hear the birds," he says. During the summer, Lynn and Alan welcome visits from their kids and grandkids, feeding the crowd with backyard vegetable garden bounty, including Lynn's famous canned tomatoes and pies made with their own tart cherries, raspberries, and apples. She also makes iced cinnamon rolls and raised donuts, which she used to make when her kids were young.

FARM FAMILY:
Claire Poupore with her sons Peter, Alan, Aaron and Scott Poupore

YEARS OWNED:
84 [since 1931]

FARMSTEAD:
4,000 acres, owned and leased

HERD:
4,200 mostly Holsteins with a few Jerseys and Norwegian Red

PAPA'S Dairy's
CHEESY BROCCOLI CASSEROLE

1   large egg

1   (10 ¾-oz.) can condensed cream of mushroom soup

½   cup mayonnaise

1   small onion, chopped

1   (16-oz.) bag frozen cut broccoli, thawed, or 1 lb. fresh broccoli florets, steamed briefly just until tender

1½   cups (6 oz.) shredded sharp or extra sharp Cheddar

1   sleeve round buttery crackers, such as Ritz, coarsely crushed

4   Tbsp. butter, melted

PREHEAT oven to 350°. Lightly coat a 13- x 9- inch baking dish or large cast-iron skillet with cooking spray (omit spray if skillet is already seasoned).

LIGHTLY beat egg with a fork in a large bowl. Whisk in soup, mayonnaise, and onion. Stir in broccoli and Cheddar.

SPREAD mixture evenly in prepared baking dish or skillet. Mix crackers with butter in a small bowl, and sprinkle evenly over broccoli mixture.

BAKE 45 minutes to 1 hour or until golden and bubbling.

MAKES 10 servings

Farmer Lynn Poupore makes this family favorite in a large cast-iron skillet handed down from her mother. She's likely to serve it as a side dish to fish on Lenten Fridays or as one of a variety of sides for large family gatherings, when her children and their families come for dinner.

CHEDDAR-STUFFED TOMATOES

Elegant and easy, not to mention delicious, baked stuffed tomatoes bring an old-fashioned touch of class to brunch, lunch, or dinner, and they pair well with everything from meatloaf to roast chicken. For even more flavor, try Tomato Basil or Garlic & Herb Cheddar in the tomato stuffing.

4   large ripe tomatoes
1   tsp. table salt, divided
2   Tbsp. butter
½   cup finely chopped onion
2   tsp. minced garlic
2   cups fresh breadcrumbs (from about 4 slices firm white bread)

1   cup (4 oz.) shredded sharp or extra sharp Cheddar
¼   cup chopped fresh parsley
¼   tsp. freshly ground black pepper

PLACE rack in upper third of oven, and preheat oven to 400°. Lightly butter a shallow baking dish large enough to hold 8 tomato halves.

CUT tomatoes in half crosswise. Scoop out and discard seeds with a teaspoon. Lightly salt interiors with about ¾ tsp. salt, and set upside down on paper towels to drain.

MEANWHILE, melt butter in a skillet set over medium heat. Add onion and garlic, and stir until onion is translucent, about 5 minutes. Increase heat to medium-high, add breadcrumbs, and continue stirring until crumbs are golden, about 5 minutes longer.

TRANSFER crumb mixture to a medium bowl, and stir in Cheddar, parsley, remaining ¼ tsp. salt, and pepper. Place tomato halves in prepared dish, and divide filling evenly among them.

BAKE about 15 minutes or until tomatoes are tender and filling is lightly browned on top.

MAKES 4 servings

GRILLED CORN SALAD
WITH SPICY CHEDDAR DRESSING

6   large ears fresh corn, husks and silk removed

6   Tbsp. extra virgin olive oil, divided

1   large or 2 medium-size red bell peppers

½   cup (2 oz.) shredded extra sharp or Artisan Reserve Cheddar

3   Tbsp. fresh lime juice (from about 2 limes)

1   tsp. minced canned chipotle pepper in adobo sauce, plus 1 Tbsp. adobo sauce

2   garlic cloves, peeled

¾   tsp. kosher salt

¼   tsp. freshly ground black pepper

4   green onions, green and white parts, sliced

PREHEAT grill to 400° to 450° (high) heat. Rub corn lightly with 2 Tbsp. olive oil. Place on grill, turning occasionally, 10 to 15 minutes or until charred in spots on all sides. Grill bell peppers, rotating as skin becomes completely blackened, about 15 minutes. Remove corn and peppers from grill; cover peppers with plastic wrap.

WHILE vegetables are cooling, combine remaining ¼ cup olive oil, Cheddar, lime juice, chipotle pepper, adobo sauce, garlic, salt, and black pepper in a blender, and blend until smooth.

WHEN corn is cool enough to handle, stand each ear up in a large bowl. Using a sharp knife, slice off kernels from all sides into bowl.

WHEN peppers have cooled, cut in half lengthwise. Rub off and discard blackened skins (some bits can remain). Remove stem and seeds. Cut bell peppers into approximate ½-inch pieces. Add bell peppers and green onions to corn in bowl.

ADD dressing, and toss to combine. Serve at room temperature.

MAKES 6 servings

The smoky flavor of charred corn and peppers is balanced with an unusual, creamy blended Cheddar dressing. This salad goes brilliantly with burgers and barbecued chicken.

BROCCOLI SALAD WITH CHEDDAR, FENNEL, AND BACON

Crunchy broccoli, crispy bacon nuggets, and savory shredded Cheddar welcome the unexpected flavor of fennel in this fresh twist on broccoli salad.

½ cup plain Greek-style yogurt

¼ cup mayonnaise

2 Tbsp. brown mustard

2 tsp. cider vinegar

½ tsp. coarse salt

5 cups chopped raw broccoli

1 cup finely diced fennel bulb

1 cup (4 oz.) shredded extra sharp Cheddar

4 bacon slices, cooked and crumbled

1 shallot, minced

WHISK together yogurt, mayonnaise, mustard, vinegar, salt, and pepper to taste in a large bowl until smooth.

ADD broccoli, fennel, Cheddar, bacon, and shallot, and stir to coat with dressing. Serve immediately, or chill several hours as desired.

MAKES 6 servings

KITCHEN WISDOM Fennel is a crisp, aromatic vegetable with a light licorice flavor. Trim off any long stalks and feathery fronds, as well as the tough bottom of the bulb, before chopping it. You can chop the fronds to toss into this salad or to save and sprinkle on fish or chicken.

BLACK BEAN AND RAINBOW PEPPER SALAD

This crunchy, zesty, colorful salad is superfast to pull together and makes a great picnic or barbecue side dish.

1 large (29-oz.) or 2 (15-oz.) cans no-salt-added black beans, drained and rinsed

1 cup (4 oz.) ¼-inch cubes Jalapeño Light Cheddar

½ cup diced red bell pepper

½ cup diced green bell pepper

½ cup diced orange or yellow bell pepper

⅓ cup chopped red onion

6 Tbsp. olive oil

3 Tbsp. fresh lime juice

½ tsp. ground cinnamon

¼ tsp. table salt

STIR together beans, Cheddar, bell peppers, and onion in a medium serving bowl.

WHISK together oil, lime juice, cinnamon, and salt in a small bowl. Pour dressing over salad, tossing to combine. Season with salt and pepper.

MAKES 8 servings

Broccoli Salad
with Cheddar,
Fennel, and Bacon

BULGUR, CUCUMBER, AND CHICKPEA SALAD

1   tsp. coarse salt

1   cup bulgur wheat

¼   cup plain Greek-style yogurt

3   Tbsp. extra virgin olive oil

2   tsp. loosely packed lemon zest

3   Tbsp. fresh lemon juice

1   tsp. freshly ground black pepper

2   cups thinly sliced English cucumber, cut into half moons

1   (15.5-oz.) can chickpeas, drained and rinsed

3   Tbsp. chopped fresh oregano or mint, optional

Fresh mint leaves for garnish, optional

BRING 1¼ cups water and salt to a boil in a medium saucepan. Turn off heat, and stir in bulgur; cover pan, and let stand 20 to 30 minutes or until water is absorbed. Uncover and cool to room temperature (spread bulgur on a baking sheet to cool faster).

WHISK together yogurt, olive oil, lemon zest, lemon juice, and pepper in a large serving bowl. Stir in cucumber, chickpeas, cooled bulgur, and herbs, if using; toss together well.

COVER and refrigerate at least 1 hour for cucumber juices to soften bulgur further and allow flavors to meld. Season with salt and pepper after chilling. Garnish with fresh mint leaves, if using.

MAKES 8 servings

Bulgur—boiled, cracked, and dried wheat kernels traditionally used in Middle Eastern and Mediterranean cooking—is perhaps best known for its starring role in tabbouleh. It reconstitutes quickly because it is already cooked. This light but nourishing salad showcases its nutty flavor and chewy texture.

KITCHEN WISDOM Bulgur comes in fine, medium, and coarse varieties, and any of those should work fine here, depending on how chewy you want the final salad. Do not confuse bulgur with cracked wheat, which has not been precooked and will take much longer to become tender.

From left, Beth Hodge, Courtney's son Colton, and Courtney Hodge holding her daughter, Honor

Echo Farm

HINSDALE, NEW HAMPSHIRE

THE WIDE-RANGING THINGS TO FIX list posted on the wall of the barn at Echo Farm, which includes "feed bin bottom to be welded," and "global warming," might be an indication that the Hodge sisters are ambitious. The Hodge sisters were barely teenagers when their parents bought Echo Farm. Before they knew it, they were in deep. They planned on having a few sheep and horses, but not a working dairy. The family's small farm, tucked in the southwestern corner of New Hampshire, is "a 4-H project gone haywire," jokes Beth, the older of the pair. Thanks to neighbors, Beth and Courtney were introduced to 4-H and then discovered Milking Shorthorns, a distinctive red and white British dairy breed. In 1990, they bought their first five animals. "We were supposed to sell them once they were bred," Courtney explains, "but then Mom said, 'Wouldn't it be fun to milk a cow?'"

The sisters both pursued agriculture studies with the goal of bringing that knowledge back to Echo Farm. They shipped milk to the co-op from the beginning and still send the majority of what their herd produces to Cabot, but, says Beth, "We always knew we wanted to make our own product, too." It was their father, a CPA and financial planner, who "pushed for pudding," Beth recalls; their original recipe is courtesy of one of his tax clients, the owner of a Greek diner in Connecticut.

The line, called Echo Farm Puddings, includes vanilla, chocolate, butterscotch, coffee, and rice puddings, along with seasonal favorites like spiced pumpkin and maple, which are distributed all over the Northeast and shipped nationwide. Although the sisters drive the farm and pudding business, they are fully supported by their family. Courtney has two young children whose toys are scattered around the sisters' office in the room next to their parents' kitchen. "Working together as sisters works well for us," says Beth.

In addition to their farm and business, the Hodges remain involved in their local 4-H club. "It was our first taste of agriculture," says Courtney. "It helps us share our love of animals and of farming," adds her sister.

Echo Farm is a great model in many ways for aspiring young farmers: It was the first dairy farm in the country certified by Humane Farm Animal Care and the farm prioritizes innovative practices like using recycled cotton from local mills for cow bedding. An active member of the New Hampshire Farm Bureau, Beth works to share farming concerns and successes with the state legislature. Maybe some day she'll be crossing "global warming" off that list.

FARM FAMILY:
Sisters Beth and Courtney Hodge with their parents Bob and Bonnie

YEARS OWNED:
28 [since 1987]

FARMSTEAD:
36 acres

HERD:
180 Milking Shorthorns and Jerseys, milking 100.

OTHER FARM BUSINESS:
Echo Farm Puddings, sell registered show calves

AWARDS:
First certified humane dairy farm in the U.S. by Humane Farm Animal Care

Echo Farm's
AU GRATIN POTATOES
WITH CHEDDAR-STOUT SAUCE

Beth and Courtney Hodge's mom, Bonnie, is Irish, and potatoes are one of her favorite ingredients. This recipe features another famous Irish pleasure, dark beer, which infuses deep flavor into the Cheddar sauce. Porter beer also works well and makes a milder sauce.

3 medium baking potatoes (about 2 lb.), peeled and thinly sliced

3 Tbsp. butter

1 tsp. chopped fresh thyme

1 medium onion, finely chopped

3 Tbsp. all-purpose flour

1 tsp. table salt

½ cup dark beer, such as stout or porter

1½ cups milk

½ tsp. freshly ground black pepper

2 cups (8 oz.) shredded sharp Cheddar, divided

PREHEAT oven to 375°. Lightly grease an 11- x 7-inch baking dish with cooking spray. Arrange potato slices, slightly overlapping, in prepared dish.

MELT butter in a medium saucepan set over medium heat. Add thyme and onion; cook 4 minutes or until onion is tender and golden, stirring occasionally.

STIR in flour and salt. Cook, stirring constantly, 1 minute or until flour is golden; whisk in beer. Increase heat to medium-high. Bring mixture to a simmer; simmer, whisking constantly, 2 minutes. Whisk in milk, and cook, whisking constantly, 3 minutes or until slightly thickened.

REMOVE pan from heat. Stir in pepper and 1½ cups Cheddar.

POUR cheese sauce evenly over potato slices. Cover and bake 45 minutes or until potato is tender. Top with remaining ½ cup cheese. Bake, uncovered, 5 more minutes or until Cheddar is melted and bubbling.

MAKES 6 to 8 servings

FIRECRACKER SMASHED POTATOES

1 large garlic bulb

1 tsp. olive oil

Pinch of coarse salt

3 lb. russet potatoes, scrubbed and cut into chunks

2 cups (8 oz.) shredded Jalapeño Light Cheddar

2 Tbsp. chopped canned chipotle pepper in adobo sauce

Sliced canned jalapeño peppers, optional

PREHEAT oven to 350°. Slice top of garlic bulb horizontally just enough to expose tops of cloves. Set on a large square of aluminum foil, root side down, and drizzle with oil. Gather foil around garlic, twisting top to close tightly. Bake 55 to 60 minutes or until pulp is golden and very soft. When cool enough to handle, break apart bulb and squeeze pulp from each clove into a small bowl; mash to puree with a fork.

BRING a large pot of water and salt to a boil. Add potatoes and cook until tender, about 20 minutes. Drain well and return to pot.

ADD Cheddar, chipotle pepper, and garlic puree. Mash to combine, leaving potatoes chunky. Garnish with jalapeño peppers, if using.

MAKES 6 to 8 servings

Whether mashed or smashed, a big bowl of creamy mashed potatoes pleases almost everyone. This version heats things up with some spicy and smoky jalapeño and chipotle peppers.

TRY SOMETHING *different*

For Greek-style yogurt mashed potatoes, start with 2 lb. cooked Yukon gold potatoes, and mash in 3 Tbsp. butter or extra virgin olive oil, 2/3 cup plain Greek-style yogurt, and 1/3 cup milk, whisked together and warmed slightly. Season with salt and pepper.

For Horseradish Cheddar mashed potatoes, start with 2 lb. cooked russet potatoes, and mash in 1/2 cup diced butter, 1/2 cup warmed light cream, 1/2 cup sour cream, and 1/2 cup shredded Horseradish Cheddar. Season with salt and pepper.

For Cheddar-chive mashed potatoes, start with 2 lb. cooked russet potatoes, and mash in 2 Tbsp. butter, 1/2 cup warmed half-and-half or milk, 2 1/2 cups shredded sharp or extra sharp Cheddar, and 3 Tbsp. snipped chives. Season with salt and pepper.

Laurel Brook Farm's POTATO ROMANO

This recipe is another one of many go-to specialties from Dottie Jacquier, beloved matriarch at Laurel Brook Farm *(see profile on page 158)*. The crunchy and slightly sharp bits of onion provide a nice balance within the rich, soft potato mixture.

Butter

3 lb. all-purpose potatoes (about 7 medium), peeled and cubed

2 cups cottage cheese

2 cups finely chopped onion

1 cup sour cream

1 tsp. table salt

1 cup (4 oz.) shredded sharp Cheddar

¼ tsp. paprika

Chopped fresh cilantro for garnish, optional

PREHEAT oven to 350°. Butter a 2- to 2½-qt. baking dish. Place potatoes in a Dutch oven; cover with cold water. Bring to a boil; boil 10 minutes or until tender. Drain.

COMBINE cottage cheese, onion, sour cream, and salt in a large bowl. Add potatoes, stirring gently.

SPOON potato mixture into prepared dish. Top with Cheddar; sprinkle with paprika.

BAKE 30 to 35 minutes or until golden. Garnish with chopped fresh cilantro, if using.

MAKES 8 servings

NEW ENGLAND POTATO SALAD WITH HORSERADISH CHEDDAR

2   lb. baby red potatoes,
    cut into 1-inch chunks

1   Tbsp. plus 1 tsp. cider vinegar

½   cup plain Greek-style yogurt

3   Tbsp. mayonnaise

¾   tsp. table salt

¼   tsp. freshly ground pepper,
    preferably white

1   cup (4 oz.) shredded Horseradish
    Cheddar

1   cup finely chopped celery

¼   cup minced red onion

3   Tbsp. chopped fresh herbs, such as
    parsley, chives, chervil, basil, tarragon,
    or dill

BRING several inches of water to a boil in a large saucepan fitted with a steamer basket over high heat. Add potatoes to steamer, and cook until flesh feels tender when pierced with a fork, about 15 minutes.

TRANSFER potatoes to a large bowl. Drizzle vinegar over potatoes, and toss to coat. Refrigerate until chilled, about 1½ hours.

WHISK yogurt, mayonnaise, salt, and pepper together in a medium bowl. Stir in Cheddar, and mix to distribute. Stir in celery, onion, and herbs. Stir yogurt dressing into potatoes, and season with salt and pepper.

MAKES 8 servings

Greek-style yogurt takes the place of much of the mayonnaise in this punchy, lightened up version of potato salad with a nice spike of flavor from Horseradish Cheddar.

ROTINI AND PEPPER JACK SALAD WITH LEMON VINAIGRETTE

With crisp and tender sugar snap peas or green beans, crunchy red onion, and nuggets of spicy cheese, this pasta salad delivers great taste and lots of texture.

½ cup thinly sliced red onion

8 oz. sugar snap peas or fresh green beans, ends trimmed and cut into 2-inch lengths

2 cups (8 oz.) uncooked rotini

1 cup (4 oz.) finely diced Pepper Jack Light or Jalapeño Light Cheddar

⅓ cup coarsely chopped fresh flat-leaf parsley

1 medium garlic clove, peeled

1 tsp. kosher salt

1 tsp. firmly packed lemon zest

¼ cup fresh lemon juice

1 tsp. Dijon mustard

½ tsp. freshly ground black pepper

3 Tbsp. extra virgin olive oil

COVER red onion with ice water in a small bowl, and set aside.

BRING a large pot of salted water to a boil; add sugar snap peas or green beans, and cook 2 to 5 minutes or until crisp-tender. Keep water boiling, but remove vegetables with a slotted spoon to a colander, and rinse under cold water until cool. Transfer vegetables to a large serving bowl.

ADD rotini to boiling water, and cook 10 minutes or until just tender. Drain pasta, rinse until cool, and add to sugar snaps or beans. Squeeze excess water from soaked onion, and add to bowl, along with cheese and parsley.

COARSELY chop garlic on a cutting board; sprinkle with salt. Mash garlic and salt into a coarse paste using a large knife blade held sideways. Scrape into a small bowl.

ADD lemon zest, lemon juice, mustard, and pepper to small bowl, and whisk until smooth. Gradually add olive oil, whisking until dressing is smooth and emulsified.

POUR dressing over salad, and toss gently until well combined. (If not serving immediately, refrigerate pasta mixture and dressing separately, and mix when ready to serve.)

MAKES 6 to 8 servings

Richardson Family
Farm's Lemon-
Yogurt Pound Cake,
page 232

Sweet Rewards

DESSERTS AND ANYTIME TREATS

"My husband and son love their dessert.
I make one every day. They'd eat it three times
a day if they could."

—Mellori Worthen, Worthen Dairy Farm,
Mercer, Maine

Missisquoi Valley Farm's MAPLE CHEESECAKE

Pauline and Jacques Couture (*see profile on page 18*) run a large maple sugaring operation on their dairy farm and are experts at cooking with all things maple, from maple sugar— the original storable form of maple before refrigeration— to syrup. They also make candy from scratch.

1⅓ cups graham cracker crumbs (1 sleeve or 9 whole cracker sheets)

4 Tbsp. butter, melted

¼ cup granulated maple sugar or white sugar

3 (8-oz.) packages cream cheese or Neufchâtel, softened

4 large eggs

1 cup maple syrup, preferably darker grade

PREHEAT oven to 350º. Wrap bottom and sides of a 9- or 10-inch springform pan with aluminum foil (to prevent leakage while baking), and coat interior with cooking spray.

STIR together crushed graham crackers, melted butter, and sugar; press mixture on bottom and partly up sides of prepared springform pan.

PUT cream cheese or Neufchâtel into bowl of an electric mixer. Add eggs, 1 at a time, beating at medium speed just until yellow disappears, scraping down sides of bowl as necessary. Add maple syrup, and blend until combined.

POUR batter into crust. (To ensure the top of the cheesecake does not crack, you can place cheesecake in a large roasting pan, and add boiling water partway up sides before baking.)

BAKE 45 to 55 minutes or until there is just a slight jiggle at the center. Remove cheesecake from oven; gently run a sharp knife around edge of cheesecake to loosen. Cool completely on a wire rack. Cover and chill 4 hours. Remove sides of pan.

MAKES 12 servings

KITCHEN WISDOM

When baking with pure maple syrup, a darker amber grade of maple will deliver stronger maple flavor than a light golden grade, which is better saved for drizzling over pancakes.

Krebs Organic Dairy Farm

STARKS, MAINE

IT'S NOT EVERY DAY you come upon a farmer with bright blue hair cuddling a bull calf, or a 77-year-old farm matriarch scraping out the barn. At Krebs Organic Dairy Farm, the family takes farming very seriously but they also know how to have fun. Darlene Taylor's blue hair was only temporary, the result of an April Fools' prank she played on her son's Cub Scout troop, but the time she spends socializing the farm's new calves is regular practice, as are the daily chores done by her mother, Marcia Krebs, every morning and afternoon, no matter the weather.

Marcia's son, David, and his wife, Billie Jo, run the farm with the help of family and a nighttime helper. Their four kids pitch in along with David's sister Darlene and her son. If family history is any indication, they'll all be working together for many years to come. Marcia's mother lived to be 101 and her dad to 96. "She says it's all the farming life," Billie Jo shares with a smile.

Tommy, David and Billie Jo's 15-year-old, is already sure of his commitment to the family business. Summer is his favorite time of year, he says, because he gets to work on the farm all the time. When asked why he likes farming, the young man immediately responds that he likes the cows. "They're generally nicer than humans," he says.

When David first took over the farm, he planned to increase the milking herd to 600, but "I got to 100 cows and wasn't liking it any more," he recalls. The farm is back to milking about 55 and grows much of its own feed. Everyone still works very hard, but there's time for snowmobiling in the woods with the kids and swimming in the stream.

"We truly believe that farming is one of the best ways to live," says Billie Jo, who welcomes tours of local schoolchildren and travels regularly to dairy group meetings. "Our kids have learned to respect their food; farming teaches them there is more to it than just going to the grocery store. It helps them appreciate what they get."

In addition to her Blueberry-Lemon Cheesecake Squares, Billie Jo often serves vegetarian Shepherd's Pie with double layers of carrots, peas, and cream-style corn, or her famous mac and cheese with no less than seven different kinds of cheese. "Someone came all the way from Bangor 70 miles away for the Cabot Open Farm Day just for my mac and cheese!" she says with a mix of pride and amazement.

FARM FAMILY:
Marcia Krebs with her daughter Darlene Taylor, son David and his family

YEARS OWNED:
36 [since 1979]

FARMSTEAD:
More than 400 acres

HERD:
Mixed herd of 150 Holsteins and Jerseys with a few Normandies

Krebs Organic Dairy Farm's
BLUEBERRY-LEMON CHEESECAKE SQUARES

1¼ cups graham cracker crumbs
(1 sleeve or 9 whole cracker sheets)

3 Tbsp. sugar

3 Tbsp. butter, melted

1 Tbsp. firmly packed lemon zest
(from about 1 to 2 lemons)

3 Tbsp. fresh lemon juice
(from about 1 to 2 lemons)

1 cup sugar

4 (8-oz.) packages cream cheese,
softened

1 cup sour cream

4 large eggs

2 cups (about 1 pt.) fresh or frozen
Maine wild blueberries

PREHEAT oven to 325°. Line a 13- x 9-inch baking dish with aluminum foil, allowing foil to extend 1 inch over edge of dish. Lightly grease foil with cooking spray.

STIR graham cracker crumbs, 3 Tbsp. sugar, and butter together in a small bowl. Press mixture into bottom of prepared dish. Bake 10 minutes. Cool completely on a wire rack (about 1 hour).

BEAT lemon zest, lemon juice, 1 cup sugar, and cream cheese at medium speed with an electric mixer until blended. Add sour cream, and beat until blended. Add eggs, 1 at a time, beating at low speed just until yellow disappears.

GENTLY stir in blueberries. Pour batter over crust, and spread evenly.

BAKE 40 minutes or until center is almost set. Turn oven off. Let cheesecake stand in oven, with door closed, 15 minutes.

REMOVE cheesecake from oven, and cool completely on a wire rack. Cover and chill 4 hours. Lift cheesecake and foil out of dish. Peel edges of foil away from cheesecake. Cut cheesecake into squares.

MAKES 24 servings

This luscious cheesecake is baked in a rectangular pan, making it very easy to serve to a crowd, as Billie Jo Krebs has done at Cabot co-op meetings. It features sweet wild blueberries, which ripen in August, but you can also use cultivated blueberries. Billie Jo credits her mom, Carolee Hand, the family baker, with the recipe.

Liberty Hill Farm's
FUDGY YOGURT TORTE

Another crowd-pleaser from Beth Kennett (_see profile on page 74_), which she serves to guests staying at the farm, as well as family and friends. Greek-style yogurt makes for a moist and rich cake, and an easy and delicious frosting.

Cake

Butter

⅔ cup all-purpose flour

⅓ cup unsweetened cocoa

1 tsp. baking powder

⅛ tsp. table salt

1½ cups sugar

⅔ cup vanilla or strawberry Greek-style yogurt

5 large eggs

1¼ cups chopped walnuts or pecans, optional

Frosting

½ cup semisweet chocolate morsels

⅓ cup vanilla Greek-style yogurt, at room temperature

PREPARE CAKE: Preheat oven to 350°. Butter a 10-inch springform pan. Whisk together flour, cocoa, baking powder, and salt in a large bowl.

WHISK sugar, yogurt, and eggs into flour mixture until batter is smooth. Stir in nuts, if using. Spoon batter into prepared pan.

BAKE 35 minutes or until a wooden pick inserted in center comes out clean. Cool cake completely in pan (about 45 minutes). Run a knife around edge of cake to loosen. Remove sides of pan.

PREPARE FROSTING: Place chocolate morsels in a small microwave-safe bowl. Microwave at HIGH 1 minute, stirring after 30 seconds; stir until smooth. (Alternatively, melt morsels in the top of a double-boiler just until they are barely melted but whisk together smoothly.)

WHISK in 2 Tbsp. yogurt until blended. Whisk in remaining yogurt. Swirl frosting over top of cake.

MAKES 10 servings

Richardson Family Farm

HARTLAND, VERMONT

From left (front): Gordon, Pat, Amy, Scott, Reid, and Audrey. On hay bale: Reid and Audrey's daughters Matilda and Priscilla and Amy and Scott's youngest son, Elliott Richardson

GORDON RICHARDSON HAS WORKED his whole life on the family's century-old farm tucked into the rolling hills of central Vermont, where the herd of caramel-colored Jerseys gazes calmly at visitors through long lashes. These days Gordon is stepping back, happy that two of his sons, Scott and Reid, have taken the lead. "He likes to say he's working his way up to feeding cats," notes Gordon's wife, Pat, with a chuckle.

In addition to the dairy, the family runs a significant maple operation with more than 8,000 taps and a sugarhouse surrounded with firewood stacked with artful prac-ticality. They also produce split-rail fencing using native wood from all over Vermont that they sell around the Northeast, including to their high-profile neighbor (and fellow co-op member), the historic Billings Farm and Museum in Woodstock. This combination has enabled the farm to support the expanding family and allowed the brothers to raise their own kids with deep connections to the land and way of life they both treasure despite its challenges. "They definitely see us working hard for what we have," Scott says. "I hope they also see I'm happy even though I'm some-times frustrated, and, as the boys say, I always smell like silage and worse."

Reid has vivid memories of going with his dad to work in the woods after spending a morning with his grandmother picking peas from the garden. "When we'd come home for supper," he recalls, "she'd cook cheeseburgers on the outdoor stone fire-place and serve them with her green tomato relish on homemade buns." For him, he says, the farming life represents "the freedom to do the things you want to do."

When Scott first met his wife, Amy, in college, she knew that he came with a farm. "That was kind of the deal," she recalls. She gradually took over the evening milking, in the early years with their three boys in a backpack or stroller. "I'm not a fancy cook," says Amy, "but I make everything from scratch: pizza, pie crust, chocolate pudding, brownies." She also works on farm-to-school education programs that help all the community's children learn the delicious value of food grown by their neighbors. The family eats their own beef, chicken, eggs, pork, lamb, milk, and vegetables and fruits. Dinner might be pizza topped liberally with garden veggies and mozzarella, or potato soup with farm corn and kale plus sausage or bacon from their pigs. They churn fresh maple ice cream from rich Jersey cream and dark swirls of their syrup and, like many sugar makers, they're much more likely to sweeten their tea and coffee with a drizzle of maple than with a spoonful of sugar.

FARM FAMILY:
Pat and Gordon Richardson with Gordon's sons Scott and Reid and their families

YEARS OWNED:
110 [since 1905]

FARMSTEAD:
450 acres

HERD:
120 Jerseys

OTHER FARM BUSINESS:
Maple, split-rail fencing

AWARDS:
Green Pastures Vermont Dairy Farm of the Year 2009, Vermont Century Farm, Vermont Outstanding Maple Family 1987, Dairy of Distinction, many Jersey breeder awards

Richardson Family Farm's
LEMON-YOGURT POUND CAKE

With three active teenage boys, Amy Richardson always has an appreciative audience for her baked goods; her youngest son is developing his own reputation for killer from-scratch brownies and biscotti. This lovely, citrusy cake is especially delicious with a cup of tea.

3 cups granulated sugar, divided

1 cup butter, softened

2 Tbsp. grated lemon zest (from about 3 to 4 lemons)

6 Tbsp. fresh lemon juice (about 3 lemons), divided

6 large eggs

2½ cups all-purpose flour, plus more for dusting

1 tsp. table salt

½ tsp. baking soda

½ tsp. baking powder

1 cup plain Greek-style yogurt

¾ cup powdered sugar

PREHEAT oven to 325°. Lightly butter and flour a 12-cup Bundt pan; chill.

BEAT together 2½ cups granulated sugar, butter, and lemon zest at medium speed with an electric mixer 4 to 5 minutes or until fluffy. Add ¼ cup lemon juice; beat until blended. Add eggs, 1 at a time, beating just until yellow disappears.

WHISK together flour, salt, baking soda, and baking powder in a medium bowl. Add to butter mixture alternately with yogurt, beginning and ending with flour mixture. Beat at low speed just until blended after each addition.

POUR batter into prepared pan. Bake 1 hour and 5 minutes or until a long wooden pick inserted in center comes out clean. Cool cake in pan on a wire rack 1 hour. Transfer cake to a plate, and cool completely (about 1 hour).

WHISK together powdered sugar and remaining 2 Tbsp. lemon juice until smooth. Drizzle glaze over cake.

MAKES 12 servings

CREAM CHEESE
MARBLED CHOCOLATE BROWNIES

2   oz. cream cheese, softened

¾   cup 2% reduced-fat vanilla Greek-style yogurt, divided

2¼ cups plus 2 Tbsp. sugar, divided

1   large egg yolk

1¼ cups all-purpose flour, fluffed with whisk before measuring

¾   tsp. baking powder

½   cup butter, cut into pieces

4   oz. unsweetened chocolate

2   tsp. pure vanilla extract

4   large eggs

PREHEAT oven to 325°. Coat a 13- x 9-inch baking dish lightly with cooking spray.

BEAT together cream cheese and ¼ cup yogurt in a small bowl at medium speed with an electric mixer until completely smooth. Add 2 Tbsp. sugar and egg yolk, and beat until blended; set aside.

WHISK together flour and baking powder in a small bowl.

COMBINE butter and chocolate in a large heatproof bowl; set over a saucepan of barely simmering water, and stir often until melted and combined. Remove from heat.

WHISK remaining 2¼ cups sugar into chocolate mixture, and then whisk in remaining ½ cup yogurt and vanilla. Add eggs, 1 at a time, whisking well after each addition. Whisk in flour mixture until well blended.

SCRAPE brownie batter into prepared dish. Spoon dollops of cream cheese mixture on top, and swirl with a spoon or spatula to create a marbled effect, reaching down into chocolate batter.

BAKE 50 to 55 minutes or just until a wooden pick inserted in center comes out with only a few moist crumbs attached. Cool in pan on a wire rack. Cut into squares.

MAKES 24 (2-inch) brownies

We took our favorite brownie recipe and replaced half the butter and cream cheese with Greek-style yogurt. The brownies are still deliciously moist and chocolaty, like a good brownie should be.

Conant's Riverside Farms

RICHMOND, VERMONT

FARM FAMILY:
Deb and Dave Conant with their son Ransom

YEARS OWNED:
163 [since 1852]

FARMSTEAD:
1,000 acres

HERD:
780 Holsteins

OTHER FARM BUSINESS:
Farmstand

AWARDS:
2005 Lake Champlain Farm Award, Dairy of Distinction

WHEN HER HUSBAND DIED SUDDENLY and unexpectedly in 1969, leaving Gloria Conant alone with six children age 11 to 17, there was no question of selling the farm that had been in the family for well over a century. With the help of her oldest sons and a few key employees, Gloria took over the reins at a time when it was rare for women to do so. As the years went by, she also made significant public service contributions. She was elected to the state legislature, awarded the title of National Dairy Woman of the Year, and named the inaugural inductee into the Vermont Agricultural Hall of Fame.

The beloved and highly respected matriarch also had the pleasure of seeing her eldest son, Dave, and his son, Ransom (named after her late husband), carry on the Conant farming tradition. Dave says that his mother rose admirably to the challenge life threw at her. He's happy that his son has joined him on the farm. "He has different challenges ahead of him than I faced," Dave says. "We're headed in the same direction, but he's following his own path."

Even since Gloria's passing a few years ago, Sunday night suppers and other family gatherings of at least a dozen still take place frequently. Dave's wife, Deb, admits that when she first stepped into her mother-in-law's spot in the farmhouse kitchen, she was overwhelmed by the constant stream of visitors. But now, says Ransom's wife, Alison, with admiration, "She can add an extra 20 for dinner without breaking a sweat. She's totally unflappable."

Meals are solid, home-cooked staples featuring the farm's own beef, sweet corn, and lots of dairy: chicken pie topped with biscuits; red sauced meat and veggie lasagna; spiral ham with corn quiche; chunky, creamy fish chowder; and goulash with beef, pasta, tomatoes, and cheese. Deb clearly knows what she's doing. Her son especially loves her Caribbean cornbread, sweet with pineapple and rich with butter, eggs, cream-style corn, and Cheddar. With the help of her three daughters who all live nearby, Deb also runs a farmstand, famous locally for its sweet corn and fall pumpkins. "They bring people to the farm. They help people understand what it takes to make food," she says. "It's about being open to the community and trying to be a good model," her son adds. "We need people to make food. We think we can do it pretty well and have a good life, too."

From left: Dave, Deb, Alison, and Ransom Conant

Conant's Riverside Farms' POLISH KOLACZKI

Alison Kosakowski Conant shared a traditional Polish recipe for a rich, flaky cookie that both of her grandmothers made around the holidays. Alison likes to use a fluted pastry wheel for decorative edges, and she fills her cookies with lemon curd or apricot or blackberry jam.

1½ cups butter, softened
1 (8-oz.) package cream cheese, softened
3 cups all-purpose flour

Powdered sugar
1 cup lemon curd or raspberry jam
1 large egg, beaten

BEAT butter and cream cheese together at medium speed with a heavy-duty stand mixer until blended. Gradually add flour, beating at low speed until a smooth dough forms. Flatten dough into a disk. Wrap in plastic wrap, and chill at least 1 hour.

PREHEAT oven to 350°. Roll dough into a 14-inch square on a work surface dusted with powdered sugar. Cut dough into 2-inch squares. Transfer squares to parchment paper–lined baking sheets.

PLACE ½ tsp. lemon curd or raspberry jam in center of each square of dough. Combine egg and 1 Tbsp. water. Fold 1 corner of each square over filling to center of cookie; brush folded pastry corner with egg mixture. Fold opposite corner over onto it, and pinch the two ends together at center of cookie firmly to seal.

BAKE 15 minutes or until edges are golden brown. Transfer cookies to a wire rack to cool completely (about 40 minutes). Dust with powdered sugar.

MAKES about 4 dozen

TRY SOMETHING different

For a slight twist on the family recipe that is just as flaky and slightly less rich, use 1 cup butter plus ¼ cup plain Greek-style yogurt in place of the full 1½ cups butter.

CHERRY, APPLE, AND ALMOND TURNOVERS WITH SHARP CHEDDAR

⅓ cup dried sweet or sweetened tart cherries

2 Tbsp. butter

About ½ cup sugar, divided

¾ tsp. ground cinnamon, divided

1 large, tart green apple, such as Granny Smith, diced

⅓ cup sliced almonds, toasted

½ cup (2 oz.) shredded sharp Cheddar

Pinch of table salt

2 juicy, sweet apples, such as McIntosh, peeled and quartered

About ¾ cup apple juice

1 large egg

1 Tbsp. heavy cream

1 (1-lb.) package frozen puff pastry, thawed

All-purpose flour for dusting

SOAK cherries in about ½ cup warm water to cover until soft, about 20 minutes.

MEANWHILE, combine butter, 1 Tbsp. sugar, and ½ tsp. cinnamon in a large skillet over medium-high heat; stir until butter is melted.

ADD green apple, and cook, stirring frequently, 5 minutes or until golden brown; transfer to a bowl, and set aside to cool.

DRAIN cherries, reserving soaking liquid in a cup measure. Add cherries, almonds, Cheddar, and pinch of salt to cooled apples; set aside. Combine sweet apple in a small saucepan with cherry soaking liquid plus enough apple juice to cover. Stir in ⅓ cup sugar and remaining ¼ tsp. cinnamon. Bring to a simmer, and cook 10 to 15 minutes or until apples are very tender. Drain off any excess liquid. Cool and mash; set applesauce aside.

WHISK together egg and cream in a small bowl. Lay puff pastry sheets on a lightly floured work surface, rolling out as necessary in order to cut 8 (5- x 5-inch) squares. Brush each square with some of egg mixture. Place a small dollop of applesauce in center of each square, and then top with 2 to 3 Tbsp. of apple-cherry mixture. Bring two opposite corners of pastry together, pressing together to seal, and crimp entire edge of turnover closed with a fork.

PLACE turnovers on a baking sheet. Brush tops with egg mixture, and sprinkle with remaining sugar. Refrigerate 30 minutes. Meanwhile, preheat oven to 375°.

BAKE 20 to 25 minutes or until puffed and golden brown. Serve warm or at room temperature.

MAKES 8 turnovers

This savory, flaky pastry filled with a combination of dried cherries, diced apple, nuts, and a little Cheddar nestled with homemade applesauce is courtesy of Stephanie's on Newbury, a restaurant in Boston, Massachusetts. The turnovers are perfect for a sophisticated dessert served warm with vanilla ice cream or packed for a sweet picnic treat.

APPLE PIE WITH CHEDDAR

For many farm families, it wouldn't be apple pie without a slice of sharp Cheddar on each serving. For Dottie and Robert Jacquier, of Laurel Brook Farm (see *profile on page 158*), making pie together is a long-standing tradition: She makes the crust; he peels the apples. "Pie for breakfast: That was in our marriage vows," says Dottie.

Crust

2¼ cups all-purpose flour, plus more for dusting

2 tsp. sugar

½ tsp. table salt

½ cup cold butter, cut into ¼-inch cubes

6 Tbsp. cold vegetable shortening, cut into ¼-inch cubes

5 to 6 Tbsp. ice water

Filling

6 cups peeled, cored, and thinly sliced cooking apples, such as Gala or Cortland (about 3 lb. apples)

¾ cup sugar

2 Tbsp. flour, cornstarch, or instant tapioca

¾ tsp. ground cinnamon

¼ tsp. freshly grated nutmeg

Pinch of table salt

2 Tbsp. butter

1 Tbsp. milk, optional

About 8 oz. sliced Vintage Choice, sharp, or extra sharp Cheddar

PREPARE CRUST: Whisk together 2¼ cups flour, 2 tsp. sugar, and ½ tsp. salt in a large bowl until well blended.

WORK ½ cup cold butter and shortening cubes into dry ingredients, using your fingertips until mixture resembles coarse crumbs, with no pieces larger than a pea.

SPRINKLE ice water on top, a tablespoon at a time, tossing everything together to combine. When dough holds together easily when pressed, stop adding water.

DIVIDE dough into 2 balls, and press into flat disks. Wrap in plastic wrap, and refrigerate 30 minutes.

WHEN ready to make pie, unwrap 1 disk of dough. Roll out on a well-floured surface, rotating, turning over, and sprinkling with more flour as needed, into an approximate 12-inch round. Fold in half over a rolling pin, and transfer to a 9-inch deep-dish pie plate, easing, not stretching, it into place.

PREPARE FILLING: Toss together apples; ¾ cup sugar; 2 Tbsp. flour, cornstarch, or instant tapioca; cinnamon; nutmeg; and pinch of salt in a large bowl.

SPOON apple mixture into prepared crust. Cut 2 Tbsp. butter into pieces, and place on top of apples.

ROLL out second disk of dough. Moisten edge of bottom crust with water, and place top crust over apples. Press edges of dough together, trimming excess to about ½ inch.

Tuck dough under itself, and crimp with your fingers or a fork to seal. Make several slits in top crust to allow steam to escape. Brush top with milk, if using. Refrigerate pie while preheating oven to 425° with oven rack in middle position.

BAKE 20 minutes; reduce oven temperature to 350°, and bake 35 to 45 more minutes or until crust is golden brown, apples are tender, and filling is bubbling thickly. (Cover crust with aluminum foil if browning too quickly.)

COOL to just warm, and serve warm or at room temperature topped with sliced Cheddar.

MAKES 8 servings

FRESH LIME AND ROASTED BANANA PIE

4 medium-firm, ripe bananas (not overripe or brown), divided

1¾ cups vanilla Greek-style yogurt

¼ cup firmly packed light brown sugar

1 tsp. lime zest, plus more for garnish, optional

2 Tbsp. fresh lime juice

1 envelope (2 tsp.) plain gelatin

1 reduced-fat graham cracker crust, or homemade graham cracker piecrust (see tip below)

Whipped cream

⅓ cup chopped toasted macadamia or cashew nuts, optional

PREHEAT oven to 350°. Place 3 unpeeled bananas on a baking sheet; pierce each in several places with tip of a knife. Bake 15 to 20 minutes or until skins are dark brown, flesh is soft, and liquid is bubbling from pierced slits. Remove from oven, and let cool in skins to room temperature.

PEEL cooled bananas, and place in a blender or food processor. Add yogurt and sugar, and process until smooth.

WHISK together 1 tsp. lime zest, lime juice, and 1 Tbsp. water in a small heatproof cup, and sprinkle with gelatin. Place cup in a saucepan filled with about ½ inch water. Set pan over medium heat. When water begins simmering, stir gelatin mixture until gelatin is completely melted. Scrape gelatin mixture into banana mixture, and process until combined.

POUR filling into crust, smoothing top. Lightly coat a piece of plastic wrap with cooking spray, and invert over top of pie. Refrigerate a few hours or until set.

WHEN ready to serve, dice remaining banana. Top each serving with whipped cream, diced banana, and a sprinkle of nuts, if using. Garnish with remaining lime zest, if using.

MAKES 10 servings

For a pie from a completely different climate, try this exotically tropical twist with flavors of banana and lime. You could scatter toasted coconut flakes on top for a final island touch.

TRY SOMETHING *different*

To make a homemade graham cracker piecrust, stir 4 Tbsp. melted butter into 1¾ cups graham cracker crumbs (from 12 "sheets" or full crackers) and 3 Tbsp. sugar.

Barstow's Longview Farm's
PEANUT BUTTER DREAM PIE

As flavor combinations go, peanut butter and chocolate is hard to beat, as Shannon Barstow, the mastermind behind Barstow's Longview Farm Store and Bakery *(see profile on page 92)*, knows all too well.

12 cream-filled chocolate sandwich cookies, such as Oreos

6 peanut butter sandwich cookies, such as Nutter Butters

4 Tbsp. unsalted butter, melted

4 oz. cream cheese, softened

¼ cup smooth peanut butter

¼ cup sugar

1 tsp. pure vanilla extract

1½ cups heavy cream, plus more for garnish, optional

16 mini chocolate peanut butter cups

½ cup milk chocolate morsels

1½ tsp. vegetable oil

PROCESS chocolate sandwich cookies and peanut butter sandwich cookies into fine crumbs in a food processor. Remove to a bowl, and stir in melted butter with a rubber spatula. Use the spatula to press cookie crumb mixture into bottom and up sides of a 9-inch pie plate. Put crust in refrigerator to chill.

MEANWHILE, cream together cream cheese, peanut butter, sugar, and vanilla at medium speed with an electric mixer until completely smooth. Whip heavy cream to soft peaks, and fold gently into cream cheese mixture, starting with one-third of whipped cream and adding more until thoroughly incorporated.

SPREAD filling evenly in crust. Top decoratively with chocolate peanut butter cups, and chill, covered, at least 2 hours.

WHEN ready to serve, microwave chocolate morsels in a small, microwave-safe bowl 30 to 40 seconds or just until smooth when whisked. (Alternatively, melt over a double boiler.) Whisk in vegetable oil. Cool for 5 minutes. Transfer chocolate drizzle into a piping bag or a small zip-top plastic bag; if using a plastic bag, snip off a tiny corner and twist bag to use as a temporary piping bag. Pipe decorative swirls over top of pie.

GARNISH with additional whipped cream, if using, and serve immediately. Refrigerate any leftovers.

MAKES 8 servings

RASPBERRY-VANILLA YOGURT CREAM

Yogurt Cream
1   envelope (2 tsp.) plain gelatin
1   cup light cream
⅓   cup sugar
2   cups vanilla Greek-style yogurt

Raspberry Topping
1   envelope (2 tsp.) plain gelatin
2   cups fresh raspberries, plus more
     for garnish
6   Tbsp. sugar

PREPARE YOGURT CREAM: Sprinkle 1 envelope gelatin over 2 Tbsp. cold water in a small bowl, and set aside.

STIR together cream and ⅓ cup sugar in a small saucepan over medium heat, and bring to a simmer. Remove from heat, and whisk 2 Tbsp. hot cream mixture into gelatin until smooth. Scrape gelatin mixture back into saucepan of remaining cream mixture, and whisk until smooth.

WHISK yogurt into cream mixture until smooth. Pour into 6 small glasses or bowls. Cover and refrigerate until set, about 2 hours.

MAKE RASPBERRY TOPPING: While yogurt creams chill, sprinkle 1 envelope gelatin over ⅓ cup cold water in a small bowl, and set aside.

COMBINE 2 cups raspberries and 6 Tbsp. sugar in a small saucepan. Stir over medium-high heat 6 to 8 minutes or until berries have completely fallen apart and released their juices. Scrape in gelatin, stirring until melted.

FIRMLY press raspberry mixture through a strainer with a rubber spatula or wooden spoon into a small bowl, pressing out all of raspberry pulp (be sure to scrape pulp from underside of strainer). Discard seeds. Set raspberry puree aside to cool to room temperature.

WHEN yogurt creams are set, spoon about 2 Tbsp. raspberry puree on each. Chill again at least 1 hour or until puree is set. Serve garnished with whole raspberries, if using. Serve cold.

MAKES 6 servings

Similar to the fancy Italian dessert known as panna cotta (cooked cream), this simple but sophisticated dessert makes a delicious dinner party finale. Find some pretty glasses to serve it in for the best effect.

DARK CHOCOLATE AND GINGER GREEK-STYLE YOGURT ICE CREAM

This supremely creamy frozen confection with shards of dark chocolate and chewy bits of crystallized ginger makes an exotic fruity treat.

1   (3- x 1-inch) piece fresh ginger
2   cups light cream
⅔   cup sugar
⅛   tsp. table salt

7   oz. 65% to 70% dark chocolate, finely chopped, divided
1½ cups vanilla Greek-style yogurt
3   Tbsp. chopped crystallized ginger, optional

PEEL fresh ginger, and cut crosswise into thin slices. Cover ginger with water in a medium saucepan; bring to a boil, and cook 1 minute.

DRAIN ginger (reserving cooking liquid for other uses), and return it to pan. Add cream, sugar, and salt. Bring mixture to a boil over medium-high heat, stirring to dissolve sugar and salt. Remove from heat; cover pan, and set aside to steep 1 hour.

POUR warm ginger-cream mixture through a strainer, discarding ginger (or save it to put in breakfast yogurt smoothies, see page 46). Pour cream back into pan, and place pan over medium heat. Place 5.25 oz. (a heaping cupful) chopped chocolate in a medium heatproof bowl. When cream is steaming, slowly pour ¼ cup hot cream over chocolate to melt it, and whisk until blended. Add remaining hot cream by the quarter-cupfuls, whisking until fully incorporated and mixture is completely smooth. Cover and refrigerate until well chilled.

WHISK yogurt into chocolate mixture. Pour mixture into freezer container of a 1-qt. ice-cream maker, and freeze according to manufacturer's instructions. Mix in remaining chopped chocolate and crystallized ginger, if using.

MAKES 8 servings

METRIC EQUIVALENTS

The recipes that appear in this cookbook use the standard United States method for measuring liquid and dry or solid ingredients (teaspoons, tablespoons, and cups). The information on this chart is provided to help cooks outside the U.S. successfully use these recipes. All equivalents are approximate.

METRIC EQUIVALENTS FOR DIFFERENT TYPES OF INGREDIENTS

A standard cup measure of a dry or solid ingredient will vary in weight depending on the type of ingredient. A standard cup of liquid is the same volume for any type of liquid. Use the following chart when converting standard cup measures to grams (weight) or milliliters (volume).

Standard Cup	Fine Powder (ex. flour)	Grain (ex. rice)	Granular (ex. sugar)	Liquid Solids (ex. butter)	Liquid (ex. milk)
1	140 g	150 g	190 g	200 g	240 ml
3/4	105 g	113 g	143 g	150 g	180 ml
2/3	93 g	100 g	125 g	133 g	160 ml
1/2	70 g	75 g	95 g	100 g	120 ml
1/3	47 g	50 g	63 g	67 g	80 ml
1/4	35 g	38 g	48 g	50 g	60 ml
1/8	18 g	19 g	24 g	25 g	30 ml

USEFUL EQUIVALENTS FOR DRY INGREDIENTS BY WEIGHT
(To convert ounces to grams, multiply the number of ounces by 30.)

1 oz	=	1/16 lb	=	30 g
4 oz	=	1/4 lb	=	120 g
8 oz	=	1/2 lb	=	240 g
12 oz	=	3/4 lb	=	360 g
16 oz	=	1 lb	=	480 g

USEFUL EQUIVALENTS FOR LENGTH
(To convert inches to centimeters, multiply the number of inches by 2.5.)

1 in					=	2.5 cm		
6 in	=	1/2 ft			=	15 cm		
12 in	=	1 ft			=	30 cm		
36 in	=	3 ft	=	1yd	=	90 cm		
40 in					=	100 cm	=	1m

USEFUL EQUIVALENTS FOR LIQUID INGREDIENTS BY VOLUME

1/4 tsp							=	1 ml	
1/2 tsp							=	2 ml	
1 tsp							=	5 ml	
3 tsp	=	1 Tbsp			=	1/2 fl oz	=	15 ml	
		2 Tbsp	=	1/8 cup	=	1 fl oz	=	30 ml	
		4 Tbsp	=	1/4 cup	=	2 fl oz	=	60 ml	
		5 1/3 Tbsp	=	1/3 cup	=	3 fl oz	=	80 ml	
		8 Tbsp	=	1/2 cup	=	4 fl oz	=	120 ml	
		10 2/3 Tbsp	=	2/3 cup	=	5 fl oz	=	160 ml	
		12 Tbsp	=	3/4 cup	=	6 fl oz	=	180 ml	
		16 Tbsp	=	1 cup	=	8 fl oz	=	240 ml	
	1 pt		=	2 cups	=	16 fl oz	=	480 ml	
	1 qt		=	4 cups	=	32 fl oz	=	960 ml	
						33 fl oz	=	1000 ml	= 1l

USEFUL EQUIVALENTS FOR COOKING/OVEN TEMPERATURES

	Fahrenheit	Celsius	Gas Mark
Freeze Water	32° F	0° C	
Room Temperature	68° F	20° C	
Boil Water	212° F	100° C	
Bake	325° F	160° C	3
	350° F	180° C	4
	375° F	190° C	5
	400° F	200° C	6
	425° F	220° C	7
	450° F	230° C	8
Broil			Grill

INDEX

ISBN-13: 978-0-8487-4398-7
ISBN-10: 0-8487-4398-9
Library of Congress Control Number: 2014956130

Printed in the United States of America
First Printing 2015

OXMOOR HOUSE

Editorial Director: Leah McLaughlin

Creative Director: Felicity Keane

Art Director: Christopher Rhoads

Executive Photography Director: Iain Bagwell

Executive Food Director: Grace Parisi

Senior Editor: Erica Sanders-Foege

Managing Editor: Elizabeth Tyler Austin

Assistant Managing Editor: Jeanne de Lathouder

THE CABOT CREAMERY COOKBOOK

Project Editor: Emily Chappell Connolly

Editorial Assistant: April Smitherman

Assistant Designer: Allison Sperando Potter

Assistant Test Kitchen Manager: Alyson Moreland Haynes

Recipe Developers and Testers: Tamara Goldis, R.D.; Stefanie Maloney; Callie Nash; Karen Rankin

Food Stylists: Nathan Carrabba, Victoria E. Cox, Margaret Monroe Dickey, Catherine Crowell Steele

Photo Editor: Kellie Lindsey

Senior Photographer: Hélène Dujardin

Senior Photo Stylists: Kay E. Clarke, Mindi Shapiro Levine

Senior Production Manager: Greg A. Amason

CONTRIBUTORS

Writer: Melissa Pasanen

Designer: Amy Bickell

Copy Editors: Norma Butterworth-McKittrick, Dolores Hydock

Proofreader: Rebecca Henderson

Indexer: Mary Ann Laurens

Photographers: Jessica Anderson, Glenn Moody

Photo Stylist: James Herrin

Food Stylist: Katelyn Hardwick

Fellows: Laura Arnold, Kylie Dazzo, Nicole Fisher, Loren Lorenzo, Anna Ramia, Caroline Smith, Amanda Widis

TIME HOME ENTERTAINMENT INC.

Publisher: Margot Schupf

Vice President, Finance: Vandana Patel

Executive Director, Marketing Services: Carol Pittard

Publishing Director: Megan Pearlman

Assistant General Counsel: Simone Procas

Recipe Credits (*Bold numbers indicate photo credit): Aimee Fortney (Easy Moist Turkey Cheeseburgers, 139); Susan Herr (Apple, Cranberry, and Cheddar Muffins, **14**; Spiced Banana Bread, **22**; Red Pepper and Cheddar Egg Cups, **29**; Cheddar Flatbread, **70**; Bean-Cheese Spirals, 72; Pepper Jack-Artichoke Hummus, 73; Hot as a Torch! Jalapeño Poppers, 77; Cheddar Cheese Straws, 78; Broccoli-Cheddar Soup, 84; Tomato-Cheddar Soup, **89**; Cheddar-Ale Soup, **90**; Lentil-Veggie Soup with Cheddar Croutons, **97**; Cheddar Soda Bread, 109; Eggplant and Chickpea Stew with Cheddar Dumplings, **112**; Meatballs Marinara with Cheddar-Spinach Polenta, **116**; BBQ Pork Burgers with Bacon and Monterey Jack, **137**; Baked Macaroni and Cheddar, **150**; Beer-Marinated Pork Tenderloin with Charred Corn-Cheddar Relish, 166; Spinach, Cheese, and Ham Cannelloni, **172**; Fish Tacos with Yogurt Crema and Mandarin-Avocado Salsa, **183**; Cheddar-Stuffed Tomatoes, **200**; Grilled Corn Salad with Spicy Cheddar Dressing, **203**; Bulgur, Cucumber, and Chickpea Salad, **206**; Rotini and Pepper Jack Salad with Lemon Vinaigrette, **218**; Cream Cheese Marbled Brownies, 235; Cherry, Apple, and Almond Turnovers with Sharp Cheddar, 240; Apple Pie with Cheddar, 242; Fresh Lime and Roasted Banana Pie, 245; Raspberry-Vanilla Yogurt Cream, 249; Dark Chocolate and Ginger Greek-Style Yogurt Ice Cream, **250**); Brianne Izzo (Baked Cauli-Nuggets, 193); Regan Jones (Whole Grain Get-Up-and-Go Bars, **17**; Pimento Cheese, **63**; Nectarine and Bacon Jam, 122; Bacon Jam, 125; Butternut Squash and Sage Bisque, **98**; Easy Artichoke Pizza Pocket, **173**); Candace Karu (Smoky Chipotle and Chorizo, 122); Jimmy Kennedy (The Ver-Monte Cristo, 128; Simple Salmon Cakes with Greek-Style Yogurt, 186); Jenn Laughlin (Sweet Potato and Black Bean Tortilla Rollups, 146); Josh Rollins (Garganelli Mac and Cheese with Roasted Jalapeños and Bacon, 157); Meg Steffy Schrier (Vegetable Tart with Cheddar Cornmeal Crust, 175); Rebecca Scritchfield (Yogurt Curry Deviled Eggs, 67; Vegetable and Cheddar Strata, 41; Savory Herb Corn Muffins, 106; Black Bean Veggie Burgers, 140); Katie Webster (smoothies on 46–47; Hot Italian Cheese Dip, **54**; Apple-Cheddar Mini Phyllo Quiches, 80; Griddled Rachel Sandwiches, **131**; Portobello Alpine Beef Burgers, **142**; Macaroni and Cheese with Butternut Squash, 153; Grilled Cheesy Portobello Caps with Turkey and Sage, **163**; Roasted Chicken Sausage with Potatoes and Apples, **164**; Cheddar Green Bean Casserole, **194**; New England Potato Salad with Horseradish Cheddar, 217; Sweet Potato–Cheddar Soup with Chipotle, 91; Broccoli Salad with Cheddar, Fennel, and Bacon, 204); University of Vermont (University of Vermont's Cream Cheese Sandwich, 122)

Additional Photo Credits: Susan Herr (Savory Herb Corn Muffins, 107; The Ver-Monte Cristo, 129; Easy Moist Turkey Cheeseburgers, 138; Black Bean Veggie Burgers, 141; Roasted Vegetable Tart with Cheddar-Cornmeal Crust, 174; Simple Salmon Cakes with Greek-Style Yogurt, 186); Glenn Moody (North African Smoky Eggs, 32; Bean-Cheese Spirals, 72; Creamy Cheesy Cauliflower Soup, 86; Cheddar Soda Bread, 109; Corn-Cheddar Risotto with Shrimp, 119; Beer-Marinated Pork Tenderloin with Charred Corn-Cheddar Relish, 167)